The Battle of Batoche

British Small Warfare and the Entrenched Métis

Walter Hildebrandt

Studies in Archaeology
Architecture and History

National Historic Parks and Sites Branch
Parks Canada
Environment Canada
1985

Available in Canada through authorized bookstore agents and other bookstores, or by mail from the Canadian Government Publishing Centre, Supply and Services Canada, Hull, Quebec, Canada K1A 0S9.

La traduction française s'intitule **La bataille de Batoche: une petite guerre britannique contre des Métis retranchés** (no de catalogue R61-2/9-24F). En vente au Canada par l'entremise de nos agents libraires agréés et autres librairies, ou par la poste au Centre d'édition du gouvernement du Canada, Approvisionnements et Services Canada, Hull, Québec, Canada K1A 0S9.

Price Canada: $6.95
Price other country: $8.35
Price subject to change without notice.

Catalogue No.: R61-2/9-24E
ISBN: 0-660-11772-X
ISSN: 0821-1027

Published under the authority
of the Minister of the Environment,
Ottawa, 1985.

Editing and design: Jean Brathwaite.

The opinions expressed in this report are those of the author and not necessarily those of Environment Canada.

Parks Canada publishes the results of its research in archaeology, architecture and history. A list of publications is available from Research Publications, Parks Canada, 1600 Liverpool Court, Ottawa, Ontario, K1A 1G2.

CONTENTS

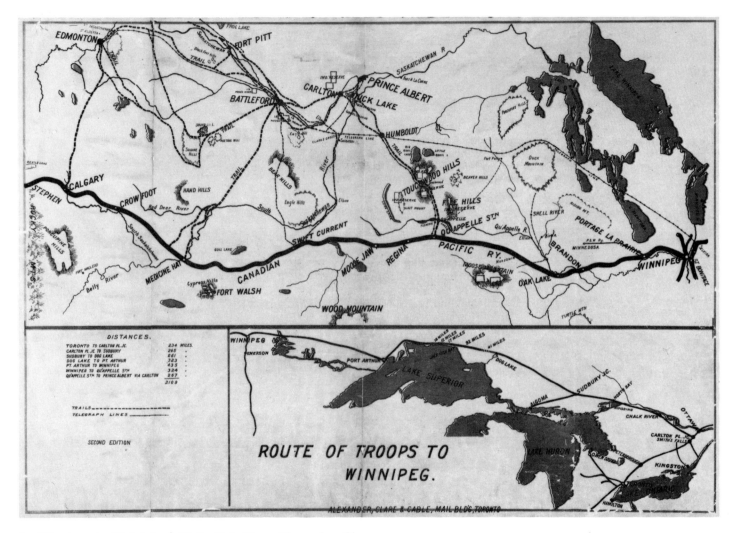

1 *Winnipeg to District of Riel's Rebellion,* Alexander, Clare
& Cable, Toronto, 1885, Second Edition. (Public Archives
Canada, NMC-24374.)

PREFACE

Mention Batoche and people think of Louis Riel, Gabriel Dumont and General Middleton, legends in Canadian history. Far less well known is what happened during the four-day Battle of Batoche. Twenty-five Canadians — whites, Indians and Métis — died there between 9 and 12 May 1885. Over a thousand men fought on the usually peaceful Canadian prairie in the largest and longest battle ever to take place in the North-West.

Maps, text and photographs are used here to relate the story of the battle. In this I am indebted to Jack Summers who gave unselfishly of his time and enthusiasm to help bring to light the course of the battle. Many times we tramped across the site to find one more part of the picture. Without his insight this could not have been accomplished. He, of course, may not agree with all I have written; any shortcomings of this work are my own responsibility.

Submitted for publication 1983, Walter Hildebrandt, Prairie Regional Office, Parks Canada, Winnipeg.

2 "Train of Red River carts meeting the York Boat Brigade," *Harper's Monthly,* June 1879. In the late 19th century most of the freighters in the North-West were Métis. (Glenbow Archives, Calgary, NA-1406-47.)

INTRODUCTION

Spring came late in 1885. Winter had been harsh. At the end of the first week of May the trees were still without leaves. Grey copses of poplar and willow surrounded by saskatoon bushes dotted the landscape, mottling the worn yellows and browns of dead prairie grasses. Life waited to break from a long winter. The cold air hung heavy with anticipation. Here at Batoche the Métis waited to defend their village and their way of life.

3 Batoche viewed from the southeast in May 1885. The man in the foreground is standing west of the church. (Public Archives Canada, C-3465.)

INTRODUCTION

In the mid-1870s many Métis had migrated northwestward from the recently formed province of Manitoba and established new communities in the North-West Territories, mainly along the thickly treed banks of the North and South Saskatchewan rivers. They left behind the confident and brash Canadian influence that was slowly moving westward, a harbinger of a new economic order planned for the West, devised in Eastern Canada and encapsulated in Prime Minister John A. Macdonald's National Policy. With the building of a transcontinental railway, prairie settlement was to follow.

Land was to be broken, grain planted, and harvests sold to foreign markets. A new, rectangular survey system was to determine settlement patterns. It was the survey and its consequences that Riel had resisted in 1869-70 at Red River, and it was from its imposition that many Métis had fled.

The families who settled along the North and South Saskatchewan represented many generations of half-breed Nor'Westers. They had established proud traditions as buffalo hunters, as provisioners for the fur trade and as trip-men and freighters throughout the North-West. Even in the 1870s the

4 The main street of Batoche included the stores of Letendre, Garnot, Boyer and Fisher. The photograph, taken in July 1885, shows some of the damage the village suffered during the battle. (Saskatchewan Archives Board, R-A 2517.)

5 François-Xavier Letendre, known as "Batoche," in 1884. Letendre was one of the most successful, and wealthiest, men in the North-West. (Saskatchewan Archives Board, R-A 12, 116.)

family names of Dumont, Ferguson, Champagne, Lépine, Riel, Gariépy, McGillis and Parenteau represented a long tradition of Métis life on the plains.

Batoche grew up at a bend in the South Saskatchewan River, 40 miles south of Prince Albert. On high ground overlooking the village the Métis built their church and rectory. The vantage point offered a beautiful view of the broad river below and the sweeping plain beyond it. The majesty of the river and the vast expanse of prairie reaching far to the distant horizon made mere mortals seem insignificant in so great a land.

On the east side of the river at Batoche the stores of Xavier Letendre, Philippe Garnot, Baptiste Boyer, Solomon Venne and Georges Fisher stood along the Carlton Trail, the principal overland route of the Métis freighters between Fort Garry and Fort Edmonton. It ran through the village, across the river and on to Fort Carlton. Villagers and travellers on the Carlton Trail and the eastern branch of the Humboldt Trail (to Prince Albert) took the ferry to the west side of the river, where the businesses of the English firm Kerr Brothers and the Prince Albert company of Walters and Baker were located. Xavier Letendre, known by his nickname "Batoche" and after whom the village was named, ran the largest and most prosperous business in the village and indeed in the whole North-West.[1] Besides being involved in freighting and fur trading, he operated a general store. The other merchants along "Batoche Avenue" owned similar establishments on smaller scales. As business grew through the late 1870s, Letendre expanded and established stores at Fort à la Corne, Carrot River, Stony Creek and Frog Lake. His prosperity was reflected in the lavish house he had built for himself and his family. Letendre's status was an indication of the stratified nature of Batoche society. It was a society distinguished between those who lived close to the land in seasonal occupations — farming, freighting, hunting and trapping — and those who were primarily merchants and businessmen.

On both sides of the river to the north and south of the village the Métis settled on river lots. Their concept of landholding had been inherited from their French-Canadian ancestors and gave each family access to the river. Their long, narrow lots stood in stark contrast to the square-grid

6 Charles Trottier *circa* 1900. He was the leader of the Métis from Round Prairie (south of Saskatoon) and brought his men to fight at Batoche. (Glenbow Archives, Calgary, NA-1036-8.)

7 Louis Letendre, Batoche's elder brother, and his wife, Angélique Dumas, *circa* 1905. (Courtesy Mme. Stella Parenteau.)

8 Jean Caron Senior and his wife, Marguerite Dumas (to the right), were photographed with their youngest son and two granddaughters *circa 1895*. The senior Caron was one of the first settlers in the area. (Parks Canada, Justine St. Germain Collection, Winnipeg.)

9 Jean Caron Junior and his mother, Marguerite Dumas, *circa 1890*. (Parks Canada, Justine St. Germain Collection, Winnipeg.)

10 Joachim Parenteau and his wife, Alphonsine, *circa* 1915. (Courtesy Mme. Stella Parenteau.)

11 Frédéric St. Germain with his wife, Melanie Parenteau, and family *circa* 1900. (Parks Canada, Justine St. Germain Collection, Winnipeg.)

survey, modelled on the American style of land division, that the federal government was undertaking. The dispute over the pattern of landholding eventually became the focal point of Métis grievances with the federal government and, more broadly, with the encroaching alien society.

Unrest broke into war in the spring of 1885. The Métis began actively resisting federal government policies. The government seemed insensitive to their longstanding complaints and they therefore prepared to bargain from a position of strength — with hostages to make their arguments more persuasive — as they had done successfully at Red River 15 years earlier.

To bargain from strength the Métis needed guns and ammunition, and they knew they could find them at Duck Lake. On 26 March the North-West Mounted Police, aware of the possibility of a Métis raid, tried to seize the ammunition and supplies before the Métis could. As they moved toward Hillyard Mitchell's store they were stopped by a group of Métis. Outnumbered, they were forced to turn back to Fort Carlton. A little more than an hour later, led by Superintendent Leif Crozier and with reinforcements bringing their contingent to 100 men, the police returned to Duck Lake, but the Métis had prepared to intercept them. On the partly frozen road 300 Métis waited. The Métis, led by Gabriel Dumont, their "Commanding General," stopped Crozier at an incline of the road as it sloped up to the high ground they occupied. Leaders of both parties met and began to parley. What happened next will never be known for certain. Someone fired a shot and a brief but bloody exchange began between the Métis and Indians hidden on either side of the road and the police, who were thrown into a panic as they realized they were caught in a crossfire. Crozier almost immediately ordered a retreat and his men tried desperately to turn their floundering horses on the snow-covered road. There were 23 victims of Métis bullets on the police side, including 12 dead, while five Métis lost their lives. The police could have been massacred had the Métis pursued them as they made their chaotic retreat, but Louis Riel, the Métis political and religious leader, who was riding around the battle scene armed only with a raised crucifix, forbade any further fighting.

12 Prime Minister Sir John A. Macdonald. (Public Archives Canada, C-5332.)

Headlines of the police's disastrous encounter with the Métis splashed across the East and greatly alarmed senior government officials. To many Victorian Easterners, the West was a lawless, dangerous frontier that needed to be tamed. The news of Duck Lake supported that image and set in motion a government determined to meet defiance by force. Prime Minister Macdonald resolved to send troops to the West as expeditiously as possible. With Adolphe Caron,

13 Sir Adolphe Caron *circa* 1886; minister of Militia and Defence from 1880 to 1891. For his part in organizing the North-West campaign Caron was made a knight commander of the Order of Saint Michael and Saint George. (Public Archives Canada, PA-12194.)

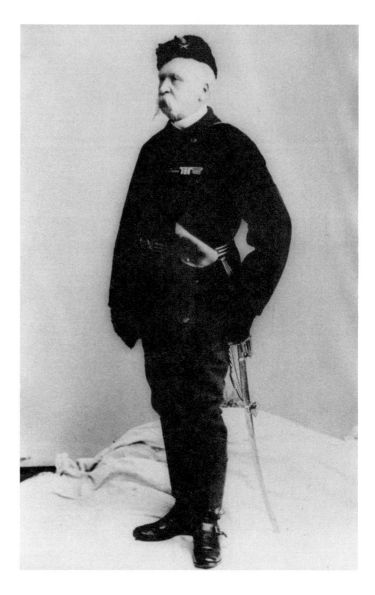

14 Major General Sir Frederick Dobson Middleton in 1885. (Public Archives Canada, PA-26732.)

his minister of Militia and Defence, and Major General Frederick Middleton, commander of the Canadian militia, he began to organize the North-West Field Force. At the time Canada had a small regular army — three corps of "permanent militia" — and a large number of volunteers in the "non-permanent" militia. To meet the demands of the North-West campaign, existing militia units were mobilized and new units were organized from as far as Halifax to suppress the "rebellion." Of the just over 5000 men mobilized for the campaign, only 400 were regular troops. Thirty-four hundred men were transported from the East, 1200 were from militia units stationed in Winnipeg, 700 were organized west of Manitoba, and the numbers were rounded out by 500 North-West Mounted Police. If needed, 1600 men waited in reserve in the East.

As the units were gathering, news of the killings at Frog Lake — where hungry Cree Indians from Big Bear's band had taken their frustrations out on the townspeople — further fed the stereotypic image of the lawless West, as did the news from Battleford, 125 miles southeast of Frog Lake, where 500 townspeople and area farmers, fearing an Indian attack, had sought refuge in the stockaded North-West Mounted Police fort. The troops were now dispatched with even greater urgency to assure that the territories would be made safe for Macdonald's dream of a settled West.

General Middleton, the commander in chief of the North-West Field Force, settled on a strategy that would send three columns up from the Canadian Pacific Railway to the major settlements in the north of the territories. Major General T.B. Strange would take one column from Calgary toward Edmonton, Lieutenant Colonel W.D. Otter would move from Swift Current to Battleford, and Middleton would advance north from Qu'Appelle to Batoche and Prince Albert. Middleton's strategy to cover as much territory as possible was essential because he did not know where the next outbreak of violence would occur.

Riel had decided to make a stand at Batoche, the place he believed would be the home of a new Catholicism. Riel steadfastly believed that divine intervention would save the Métis at Batoche. Dumont did not want to dig in there, but preferred to pursue guerilla warfare against the cumbersome

15 Louis Riel in 1878. (Manitoba Archives.)

16 Gabriel Dumont *circa* 1886-87. (Saskatchewan Archives Board, R-A 6277.)

columns of the North-West Field Force. He wanted to harass his enemy as it slowly moved into an unknown land. Wooded coulees and prairie copses would be cover from which to ambush the vulnerable army marching along winding roads. Such tactics had been proven at Duck Lake and were to be proven again at Fish Creek, but Dumont deferred to Riel and made the most of what must have appeared to him as a hopeless situation.

Unsure whether the first attack would be from the North-West Mounted Police stationed at Prince Albert or from the army approaching from the south, the Métis, under Dumont's direction, devised an elaborate defence system on all sides of Batoche. Making use of their knowledge of the land to best advantage, they dug rifle pits to cover critical points along the trails — heavily wooded areas and the narrow bridges over the many creeks in the area — and often positioned the pits at the tops of inclines in the roads to allow them to fire from concealment down at any approaching soldiers. Pits were also gouged out along the high banks on the west side of the river. All these defences would allow the Métis to attack anyone approaching on the roads or to fire across the river at exposed soldiers on the east side of the river. Another line of pits, and as it turned out, the most important one, was dug on the east side of the river at the crest of the slope above the village. Others were dug around the cemetery and along the edge of the ravine to the south and west of the church and rectory. The trails approaching Batoche from Fish Creek and Humboldt were also lined with pits. Batoche was surrounded by entrenchments; 760 acres were honeycombed with defences. Much planning and thought had gone into the strategy to defend the village.

The individual pits were often large enough to hold up to ten men and their supplies. Logs placed at the front of each pit allowed the Métis to fire through the breastworks at approaching soldiers. In most cases the pits were totally concealed and virtually impervious to bullets. Many pits had a sloped area to the rear where riflemen could slip in and out to move about the battlefield quickly and unnoticed. It was an important part of their strategy to be mobile. When they were outnumbered, mobility would allow them to meet any

17 Sketch of a Métis rifle pit by Captain Haig of the Royal Engineers. The men would use one of the square notches on the front wall as a foot rest while firing. (Glenbow Archives, Calgary, NA-2274-21.)

flanking movements that might be attempted. Batoche and its surrounds were a vast area for only 250 to 300 men to defend.[2]

The Métis were not the only ones to defend Batoche. Some Dakota (Sioux) and Cree fought beside them. Riel had hoped that English- and French-speaking whites, half-breeds and Indians would present a united front in bargaining with the government. But the whites deserted the cause when fighting with guns took over from fighting with words and petitions, and most Indians stayed away from Riel. Indian aims generally differed from those of the Métis, mistrust clouded their relations, and only a few joined Riel.

18 Big Bear *circa* 1886. Some of his Cree were among the Indians who fought in 1885 in spite of his efforts to restrain his men. (Manitoba Archives; copy from Glenbow Archives, Calgary, NA-1315-17.)

19 Poundmaker *circa* 1885. Attacked by Colonel Otter at Cut Knife Hill, his band of Cree fought the soldiers off but did not pursue the retreating column. (Public Archives Canada, PA-117947.)

20 Crowfoot *circa* 1890. The leader of the feared Blackfoot Confederacy kept his Indians out of the fighting. (Glenbow Archives, Calgary, NA-29-1.)

21 White Cap, a Dakota chief, and his daughter after the battle. (Saskatchewan Archives Board, R-B 4633.)

The Indians who did fight at Batoche were Dakota from White Cap's band and Cree from One Arrow's band. Their numbers are not precisely known, but evidence given at the trials afterward suggests that there were approximately 20 Indians with White Cap and 15 to 20 with One Arrow.[3] Both chiefs were old, both denied their guilt, and both stated that Riel forced them to participate. In White Cap's case, when 18 to 20 Métis went to his reserve and drove off his cattle, the Indians' major source of food, the Dakota followed the herd to Batoche. There, White Cap claimed, they were intimidated into fighting. White Cap was acquitted of levying war against the queen, but One Arrow was convicted.[4] One Arrow denied his guilt only after the judge had read his conviction. Up to his sentencing, One Arrow had remained silent. He claimed that his band's entire herd of cattle had been ordered slaughtered by Michel Dumas, the Métis farm instructor on the chief's reserve, and that his men were subsequently compelled to join Riel.

There were also suggestions afterwards in the testimony of the Métis that some of them, too, felt pressured into fighting.[5] When Riel warned that deserters would be shot on sight, few doubted that he meant what he said. Also, the story told was that when Riel gathered the Métis at Batoche on 19 March to celebrate the anniversary of their patron saint, Saint Joseph, they were told that 500 North-West Mounted Police were approaching from Prince Albert and that if they left the settlement, not only would their lives be endangered, but also the virtue of their women could not be protected. Nevertheless, some members of the commercial class were absent during the battle. Letendre, Fisher, Venne and others were nowhere near any of the fighting, and William and Baptiste Boyer left Batoche quietly as the fighting began. As well, there were some who doubted the soundness of Riel's theological schemes. By the time of the fighting, Riel had lost the support of the clergy, which left some of the Métis doubtful about Riel.[6] Riel and Dumont, therefore, may have used some form of coercion to convince those who were vacillating, unsure whether to take up arms.

There can be no doubt about the conviction of some of Riel's followers. Led by Gabriel Dumont, they were primarily hunters, farmers, trappers and freighters, those not directly

22 Napoléon Nault, Riel's cousin, and Napoléon Carrière *circa 1885.* (Société historique de St. Boniface, Manitoba.)

23 Maxime Lépine, one of Riel's captains, in 1875. (Manitoba Archives.)

involved with the commercial establishment. Their grievances were generally the same as the merchants'. They all resisted the survey. They all were concerned with land titles, land grants or money in lieu of land, representation on the territorial council and in parliament, and taxes levied on the "necessaries of life."[7] But these devoted men were determined to follow Riel's path wherever it led. The hard core included Damase Carrière, Isidore Dumont, Donald Ross, Norbert Delorme, Napoléon Nault, Michel Dumas, Maxime Lépine, Philippe Gariépy, Philippe Garnot and Baptiste Boucher. Many of them paid for their resistance with their lives.

Middleton faced no such divisiveness among his men. His strength lay in numbers and in the commitment of his admittedly inexperienced soldiers. Though much maligned after the campaign, Middleton represented the elite of the British officer corps and he complemented his own position by surrounding himself with other British regular officers, most notably Chief of Staff Lord Melgund and Lieutenant Colonels C.E. Montizambert and Bowen Van Straubenzie.

What stands as a remarkable achievement for the North-West campaign was the rapidity with which troops were dispatched to the theatre of war. The men were rushed to the territories along the partially completed Canadian Pacific Railway line. From the outbreak of violence at Duck Lake on 26 March it took less than a month before soldiers were in action at Fish Creek. Even more notable was the maintenance of the troops in the North-West. The presence and co-operation of the Hudson's Bay Company made transport available and ensured a food supply for both man and beast. The company, well paid for its assistance, was "indispensable" to the success of the Field Force.[8]

Weapons and ammunition gave the Field Force another advantage. The single-shot Snider Enfield rifles were not as good as the repeating, lever-action Winchesters of the Métis, but the nine-pound field guns and Gatling gun had no counterparts on the Métis side.

An important unknown was the fighting ability of the North-West Field Force, a volunteer army made up of farmers, clerks and shopkeepers. Many had never fired a shot in anger; others had never fired at all. Privately and in telegrams to Caron, Middleton had expressed doubts over the

combat potential of the unseasoned troops. His fears were confirmed at Fish Creek, 60 miles northwest of Humboldt, where the raw troops saw their first action.

The Battle of Fish Creek was fought on 24 April in a small dog-legged coulee at a point where the Fish Creek Trail slopes down across the creek. Here 200 Métis, commanded by Gabriel Dumont, waited entrenched among the scrub and trees to ambush Middleton's troops. Middleton had split his men: one group, 370 men under Lieutenant Colonel Montizambert, was moving north on the west bank of the South Saskatchewan River, and the rest of his men, under his own command, were following a parallel course along the east bank. Had Boulton's scouts not come across still-smouldering Métis campfires and alerted Middleton to caution, there would have been an awful blood bath in the gulley. Yet, even being forewarned, the North-West Field Force could not dislodge the Métis and Indian marksmen. Repeated attempts by Middleton's men to rush and clear the coulee failed. After six hours of fighting the battle ended when the Métis withdrew. Middleton counted 55 casualties, almost 25 per cent of his initial attacking force, which included six dead. The Métis had lost just four men. The battle left Middleton's confidence shaken and slowed his previously rapid advance. He regrouped, set up camp, drilled his rookie soldiers and waited for the Hudson's Bay Company steamer *Northcote* to bring reinforcements and supplies.

If the initial response of Middleton's troops to battle had just been demonstrated, greater questions were still unanswered. Whom would he be fighting? How many of the 22 000 Indians and Métis in the West would take up arms?

24 Gilbert John Elliot-Murray Kynynmound, Lord Melgund, later the fourth Earl of Minto, *circa* 1890. (Public Archives Canada, C-2487.)

How tenacious would resistance be? What would further setbacks to his recruits' morale mean? Fish Creek had shown Middleton the ingenuity of the Métis as they made use of the familiar terrain to harass his all too visible army. Would continued guerilla action cripple his vulnerable force as it moved into inhospitable territory?

What Middleton was armed with more than anything else as he faced these unknowns was the British tradition of "small warfare" applied in similar circumstances throughout the empire. To this tradition Middleton brought his own campaign experience in New Zealand, India and Burma, where he had fought equally stubborn foes.

25 Artillery practice after the battle at Fish Creek. The gunner on the right makes last-minute adjustments under the eye of the battery sergeant major standing on the left. (Public Archives Canada, C-3461.)

PART I
THE BATTLE OF BATOCHE
9–12 MAY 1885

The Manitoba treaty has not been fulfilled.... There were two societies who treated together; one was small, but in its smallness it had its rights. The other was great, but by its greatness it had no greater rights than the rights of the small.

Louis Riel, 1885.

26 The *Northcote.* (Public Archives Canada, C-3447.)

On 5 May the *Northcote* landed at Fish Creek with supplies and two companies of the Midland Battalion on board. Middleton's confidence seemed renewed with the appearance of the steamer, and he now focussed his attention on Batoche, where he knew Métis were gathered. A new determination pervaded his communications and he no longer expressed concern over a shortage of manpower. Earlier he had talked of combining forces with Lieutenant Colonel Otter's column for an attack on Batoche, but on the 5th he dropped that possibility. In part the decision was due to

27 Captain J.A. Johnston and men of Boulton's Mounted Infantry, 1885. Raised in southern Manitoba by Major Charles Boulton, a former British army officer, the unit was widely used by Middleton for scouting. While the officers wore scarlet military frockcoats, the men wore civilian work clothes Boulton bought from the Hudson's Bay Company. (Manitoba Archives.)

Otter's fall from favour after his humiliating battle with Poundmaker's Cree at Cut Knife Hill on 2 May. (Otter had embarked on his mission to Cut Knife Hill against Middleton's orders although with the approval of the lieutenant governor of the territories.[1]) The arrival of the *Northcote* and news of Otter's encounter at Cut Knife Hill were the main factors in Middleton's decision to move against Batoche. A two-pronged attack was still planned to take the village, but Otter would no longer be part of it. Middleton's own men would advance on two fronts.

It was during this time, 26 April to 4 May, that Gabriel Dumont reportedly wanted to intercept the North-West Field Force. "Many times, when Middleton ... went out into the open area, it would have been easy to decimate the troops in the ravines and [on] the flanks. And Riel never consented to let them do it."[2]

Middleton had grown anxious to proceed while awaiting the *Northcote*. He had ordered some preparations before 5 May: reconnaissance was carried out, arrangements for wounded made, and exercises conducted. On the 5th another reconnaissance of Métis positions was undertaken by Middleton accompanied by Lord Melgund, Boulton's Mounted Infantry and French's Scouts. Their route took them to a house from which a group of Métis had recently fled, leaving a still-smouldering fire. The party then came across Dumont's house at Gabriel's Crossing, on the South Saskatchewan River just 13 miles north of Fish Creek, where "the General gave orders that we could allow nothing to be touched, and turned all of the men out of the building, not, however, before some mementoes of the campaign had been secured."[3] The men also brought back 20 head of cattle.

The arrival of the *Northcote* significantly strengthened Middleton's force. On board the boat were 80 men of the Midland Battalion, Colonel Van Straubenzie, and Captain A.L. Howard, of the Connecticut National Guard, who represented an American gun manufacturer, with a sample Gatling gun. Once the steamer arrived, Middleton rapidly finalized his schedule.

Wednesday, 6 May, was spent preparing the *Northcote* for action. Middleton was planning the first use of naval warfare in the North-West. The steamer was to provide a second

28 Two sergeants and a private of the Midland Battalion raised in southern Ontario. The seated sergeant wears the old-issue Norfolk jacket, which had largely been discarded by 1885 because of its "un-soldierly" appearance. (Public Archives Canada, C-24335.)

front by attacking from the river. Apparently very few officers were aware of Middleton's plans; certainly the minister of Militia and Defence, Adolphe Caron, was not informed about them. Those in daily contact with Middleton remarked on his reluctance to share or discuss his tactics. "But nothing of the General's intention was known until the following day, and I may say here that I never met a man who was so thoroughly able to keep his own council [sic], no one knowing until orders were issued what the projects were."[4]

Alterations to the *Northcote* were made by Major Henry Smith, of "C" Company, Infantry School Corps, who had been placed in command of the steamer. Middleton ordered the upper deck to be made "bullet proof" and placed a somewhat motley crew on board: 31 rank and file and Smith and one other officer of "C" Company, Infantry School Corps; Captain S.L. Bedson, the chief transport officer; Captain H.G. Wise, Middleton's aide-de-camp; Mr. Magre and Mr. Pringle, medical staff; several men of the supply and transport services; Mr. Gottam, a newspaper correspondent; and a few settlers. In all there were approximately 50 combatants on board in addition to the civilian crew.[5] Loading down a steamer that had already experienced serious difficulties with sandbars was impractical.

> The commander had conceived the rather ludicrous idea of converting the *Northcote* into a gunboat. She was furnished with clumsy barricades, which were to serve as bulwarks, and as she had no cannon to counter against, the task of rendering these barricades bullet proof was not a difficult one. The utter folly of equipping and arming her in the manner described was seen when she passed down the river and began the fight on May 9.[6]

Finally, on 7 May, Middleton was prepared to move. The general had 886 men (all ranks) in addition to the men on the *Northcote*:

Boulton's Mounted Infantry	70
French's Scouts	29
"A" Battery, Regiment of Canadian Artillery	101
Winnipeg Field Battery	58
10th Royal Grenadiers	258

29 Rifleman Robert Kellock Allan, on right, and a fellow member of the 90th (Winnipeg) Battalion of Rifles *circa 1885.* Both have Snider Enfield rifles. (Glenbow Archives, Calgary, NA-2381-1.)

90th (Winnipeg) Battalion of Rifles	270
Two companies, Midland Battalion	100[7]

(The Infantry School Corps and the Regiment of Canadian Artillery were the only regular troops with Middleton.) Lieutenant Colonel Van Straubenzie's arrival on the *Northcote* had prompted a reorganization of those men and officers. Van Straubenzie was placed in command of a small infantry brigade consisting of the 10th Royal Grenadiers, the Winnipeg Rifles and the Midlanders. According to Lord Melgund, the chief of staff, the headquarters staff was:

Commander in Chief: Major General Sir F. Middleton
Chief of Staff: Lord Melgund
Aide-de-camp: Captain H.G. Wise
Lieutenant: A.E. Doucet
Lieutenant: H.C. Freer
Commanding Artillery: Lieutenant Colonel C.E. Montizambert
Infantry Brigadier: Lieutenant Colonel Bowen Van Straubenzie
Deputy Adjutant General: Lieutenant Colonel C.F. Houghton
Acting Deputy Adjutant General: Major H. Smith
Acting Quartermaster General: Captain H. de H. Haig
Brigade Major: Captain G.H. Young
Brigade Major: C.G. Harstone
Brigade Surgeon: Dr. G.J. Orton
Brigade Surgeon: Dr. E.A. Graveley
Chief Transport Officer: S.L. Bedson
Assistant Transport Officer: J.E. Secretan
Assistant Transport Officer: Major Kirwan
Supply Officer: Mr. Underwood
Orderly Officer: Major Street
Camp Quartermaster: George F. Cole
Chief Interpreter: Mr. Hourie[8]

The troops at Middleton's disposal were predominantly infantry and were complemented by three groups of mounted infantry: Boulton's Mounted Infantry, French's Scouts and, arriving on 11 May, the Dominion Land Surveyors Intelligence Corps. There was to be no trained cavalry at the front even though Lieutenant Colonel Denison's cavalry could have been

30 Sergeant T. Wright, "F" Company, Winnipeg Rifles, after the campaign. His two medals are for marksmanship; the North-West campaign medal was not issued until 1886. His rifle is one of the few newly issued Martini Henry's given to the best shots in the battalion. (Parks Canada, Winnipeg.)

31 Captain A.L. Howard of the Connecticut National Guard with the infamous Gatling gun. (Public Archives Canada, C-1882.)

brought from Humboldt — a decision for which Middleton was later criticized.

Four field guns were available to Middleton: two with the Winnipeg Field Battery and two with "A" Battery of the Regiment of Canadian Artillery. All four were Rifled Muzzle Loading nine-pounders. Each gun had a range of 3000 yards and weighed, with its carriage, close to a ton. They were extensively used by Middleton, especially at Batoche. Their direct effectiveness against the elusive Métis and the well-hidden rifle pits might be questioned, but they were certainly effective in demoralizing the enemy and in causing extensive property damage over the four days of the fighting.[9]

More publicized than the nine-pounders was the Gatling gun carried to the front by the *Northcote*. Captain Howard operated it throughout the campaign. Its effectiveness at Batoche has been the source of some controversy. It was the first time many had ever seen a rapid-fire gun in action, and it attracted considerable attention and commentary during and after the campaign. Major Boulton was cautious in assessing the Gatling's contribution to the success of the North-West Field Force at Batoche. While admitting that it was a significant weapon, especially on the first day, he was less effusive than most. Boulton felt that the success attributed to it detracted from the brave and solid role played by the infantry and artillery companies.[10] The Métis referred to the Gatling as the "rababou" or noisemaker; they claimed it made a lot of noise but did little damage.

The advantage of the Gatling gun was primarily its rapid-fire capacity: it was advertised as being able to fire 1000 shots per minute. It was also relatively light to transport and easy to adjust for both elevation and direction when firing. The gun had ten barrels, five of which were firing in succession while the other five were being loaded, thus eliminating the time-consuming process of stopping to reload after each shot. When the crank that operated the gun was turned, firing, loading and shell extraction all took place in one uninterrupted sequence.

On the afternoon of the 7th the troops marched the 13 miles from Fish Creek to Gabriel's Crossing, which they reached by 6:00 p.m.[11] There they met the *Northcote*, which had arrived that afternoon. Middleton who "had learned there were some nasty places to pass on the river trail [from Fish Creek]," went out to decide on the safest approach to Batoche. He

> rode out with some scouts to the east, accompanied by Mr. Reid, the Paymaster of the Midlanders, etc.... With his assistance I marked out a route for next day's march which would bring us on the Humboldt trail to about five or six miles from Batoche.[12]

The North-West Field Force was now close to Batoche and Middleton was not the only one who felt uneasy in the thick bush. Some spent that evening filled with apprehension. "The night was an anxious one; we were encamped [near] Riel's stronghold, who was aware of our presence, and there was ample cover to make a night attack, with little warning."[13]

On the morning of the 8th, a Friday, the North-West Field Force began its march out of the bush toward the more open prairie. But first they again visited Dumont's house: "the troops took out a billiard table and a washing machine and put them on board the Northcote, and then fired the house."[14] The march moved east and north along the eastern branch of the Humboldt Trail between clumps of poplar and willow and patches of swampy terrain. They then turned north onto a secondary path leading to Batoche, following it for two miles before camping for the night near one of many alkaline ponds, not far from the crosstrail leading to the

32 Officers and men of the Winnipeg Field Battery, 1885. (Public Archives Canada, C-79108.)

Carrot River settlement farther east. Their position was "eight miles east and a little south of Batoche's."[15] (The next day the Field Force would return to the Humboldt Trail for the final miles of their approach to Batoche.) In the meantime the *Northcote,* which had been patrolling the riverbanks where many Métis had been spotted, particularly on the west bank, was readied for action the next morning.

Middleton made a final reconnaisance that evening. "Leaving Van Straubenzie to pitch camp, I rode forward with Boulton and his scouts to within a mile of Batoche, driving in some of the enemy's scouts."[16] On his return to camp

Middleton gathered his officers to inform them of his plan for a two-pronged attack.

Reveille was sounded at 4:00 a.m. on Saturday the 9th. Breakfast was taken at 4:15 and the men were ready to march at 5:00, each man carrying 100 rounds of ammunition. At 5:30 the advance began. The order of march was:

Advance guard, Boulton's Mounted Infantry, extended, with extended men on each flank
Main body, Boulton's Mounted Infantry
Gatling gun
Advance guard, 10th Royal Grenadiers

33 Marching order of Boulton's Mounted Infantry and French's Scouts. (Glenbow Archives, Calgary, NA-363-7.)

Main body, 10th Royal Grenadiers
90th (Winnipeg) Battalion of Rifles
"A" Battery, Regiment of Canadian Artillery; two nine-pounder field guns
Midland Battalion
Winnipeg Field Battery: two nine-pounder field guns
Ammunition wagons
Ambulance
French's Scouts[17]

Before the march began, however, an unexpected parcel arrived containing 10 000 cigars, sent out by a Montreal company. As Major Boulton wrote, "by this thoughtful act I was enabled to serve out a cigar to each man, and we marched off amidst good humour and lots of chaff."[18] Middleton was seen with his cigar later in the day during the fighting:

he was cool as the proverbial cucumber and instead of commanding an army in the field, while under the fire of a determined and well entrenched enemy, one would almost have thought by the cool and unconcerned manner in which he rode about the field, and smoked his havana cigar, that he was only superintending a brigade on a field manoeuver.[19]

9 MAY: INCAPACITATING THE *NORTHCOTE*

On the morning of 9 May the Métis and Indians neutralized part of Middleton's tactics by shaving off the *Northcote*'s smokestacks at the ferry crossing, leaving Middleton with only one front to attack and without the possibility of a landing behind Métis lines. The coordinated pincer manoeuvre was supposed to take place at 8:00 a.m. with the steamer moving downriver and Middleton's column coming overland from the southeast, but the *Northcote* reached the village too soon. There are discrepancies in the times given for the *Northcote*'s coming under fire. What is certain is that the mission aborted when the *Northcote* met resistance before 8:00 a.m. while the remainder of the North-West Field Force was still some miles from Batoche.

The use of the *Northcote* was a crucial part of Middleton's tactics. On the evening of the 7th he had ordered Major Smith to remain at Gabriel's Crossing until the morning of the 9th when, at 6:00 a.m., Smith was to move downstream. The steamer was to halt just past Batoche until bombardment from Middleton's guns was heard and then to land and disembark the troops to attack from the river side. On the 8th Smith had made further preparations on the steamer: "the vessel had been partially prepared for defence, but not, as I considered, sufficiently; so the 8th was employed in adding to the defences by piling up sacks of oats, boxes of meat, etc."[1] The *Northcote* was also towing two heavy barges loaded with supplies and fuel.

On the morning of 9 May the *Northcote* started out as planned. At 6:00 a.m. the steamer had moved to a point just above Batoche where it was anchored because it was slightly ahead of schedule. Just before 8:00, as the *Northcote* struck toward midstream to execute its part in the two-pronged attack, it came under heavy Métis fire from both banks. At first Smith's men did not return the fire, but as the bullets became heavier they began "independent and volley firing."[2] The Métis were ready for "Middleton's Navy."

We were raked fore and aft by a fierce storm of bullets coming from both banks. From almost every bush rose puffs of smoke, and from every house and tree on the top of the banks came bullets buzzing. The fire was steadily returned by the troops on board ... and notwithstanding that the rebels were protected by the brush and timber which covers the banks, apparently some injury was inflicted upon them. Volley after volley was fired, and several of the lurking enemy were seen to drop headlong down the sloping banks.[3]

Heavy fire continued as the steamer pushed on toward the village. As Middleton wrote, "as we got near the river, much to my annoyance we heard a rattling fire and the steamer's whistle, showing the latter was already engaged."[4]

Father Fourmond, who was in the rectory throughout the fighting, recalled the *Northcote*'s arrival:

around 8 a.m. we were out on the plateau of the mission, getting more and more worried.... Suddenly a terrible howl (bellow) came to my ears, coming from upstream. We look at each other: It's the steamboat. It seems like a signal. The sound gets closer and closer. No more doubt. It's the steamboat arriving and whistling war. We expected Middleton's soldiers to arrive from the prairie; we assumed an understanding between boat and army. Boat arrived in front of the mission, we see it going down and advance between the two camps [sic] along the riverbanks and force passage. No firing heard anywhere. The attack starts by a group of Sioux camped close to the mission; we see them getting rid of their blankets and leggings in haste, done very fast. Immediately take guns and run toward boat through the bushes. Hiding as best they could so not to attract the attention of the defenders of the steamboat. They were barely out of

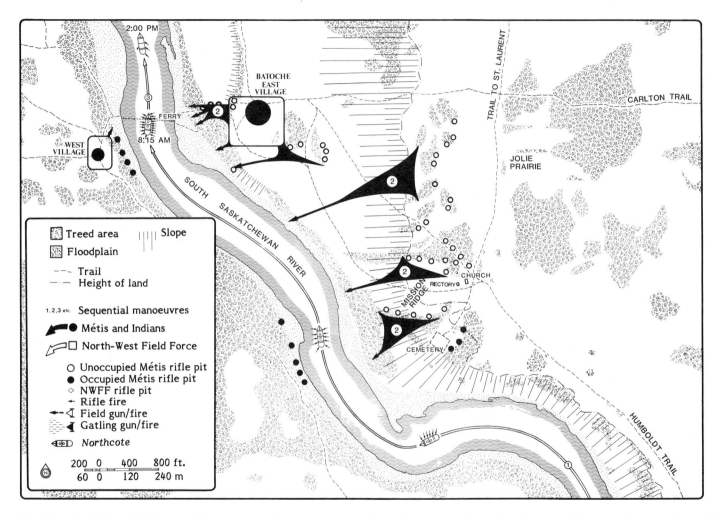

34 Day 1, 9 May, 8:00 a.m. The steamer *Northcote* passed Batoche before Middleton could reach the village overland and the two-pronged attack failed. The Métis left their rifle pits to fire on the steamer from the riverbank, and at the ferry crossing the ferry cable was lowered, sending the steamer's smokestacks crashing to the deck. (Map by B. Richard and D. Kappler.)

35 "The Steamer 'Northcote' Running the Gauntlet at Batoche...," *The Canadian Pictorial and Illustrated War News,* Souvenir Number, Pt. 2, 29 August 1885. (Saskatchewan Archives Board, R-B 7380; copy on file, Public Archives Canada.)

our sight, when we heard some gunshots, followed by many more, mixing with the sound of the boat whistle. The battle had started. The shooting became heavier as the boat came downriver and neared the camp. We feared for the poor people caught between two fires. We thought the [ferry] cable could turn it over and sink it. Watching the battle from this site, we often looked out at the prairie to see red coats, expecting every instant for the shooting to start on this side. Strangely, inexplicably, no one appeared and for about an hour only the boat was involved in the shooting.[5]

Almost all of the Métis left their rifle pits on the east side of the village to fire on the *Northcote* as it moved downriver. Philippe Garnot, one of the Métis captains, himself sent about 20 men to join the assault.[6]

The decapitation of the *Northcote*'s smokestacks was engineered by the ferryman, Alex P. Fisher, assisted by Pascal Montour. They lowered the ferry cable suspended across the river as the steamer passed, sending the stacks crashing to the deck. Smith was unaware of the loss of the stacks and whistle until after the *Northcote* anchored downstream, even though "as we passed Batoche the fire was especially heavy, and I heard a crash as if a portion of the upper deck had been carried away."[7] The Métis had wanted to stop the steamer and pour fire onto it, and though their goal was not realized, the damage was considerable:

the ferry cable caught the smoke stacks which came crashing down on the hurricane deck, tearing with them spars and masts. Our misfortune excited loud cheers from the Métis, mingled with fiendish war-whoops from the Indians. The cable which is strung from the upper banks, was lowered just as we approached it, the intention of the rebels being to corral the steamer and, in the confusion expected to ensue, to capture the boat and massacre its human freight. Very fortunately for us this scheme failed, but only by the merest chance, for had the cable caught the pilot-house, which it barely missed, the wheelsman, exposed to the enemy's fire, would have been shot down and the steamer rendered utterly helpless. It was successful, however, in cutting off our communication with

General Middleton by our code of whistling signals, previously arranged upon, the whistle being carried away with the pipes.[8]

It was also successful in crippling the steamer's engines. With the tall smokestacks gone, the updrafts were lost, the boiler fires were no longer efficient and the steam that powered the boat was reduced to a minimum.

The *Northcote* then crossed the "rapids" and barely avoided disaster: "a big rock covered with sand juts out into the stream, leaving a narrow channel immediately on the western side, the head of which is at a sharp bend, to round which the boat had to run her nozzle almost onto the bank."[9]

Misfortune followed the *Northcote* as it made its halting way, "stern aforemost for awhile." When it came to rest three miles downstream the crew, in an almost mutinous state, refused to go upstream again for fear of their lives and refused to repair the whistle. When some repair work was finally attempted, it was halted because a crew sent ashore for wood was fired on by the Métis who had followed the steamer. None of the crew would go on deck after a carpenter working in the open was hit in the heel by a bullet. (Only two other injuries — also minor — were reported on the *Northcote* during the entire episode.) As the boat continued to move downstream, it was fired upon intermittently throughout the night of the 9th. On the 10th the steamer remained anchored under light rifle fire from both banks. The next day Smith decided, after the arguments of the reluctant pilot prevailed, to move further downstream to a Hudson's Bay Company ferry landing, where the two heavy barges would be left. The *Northcote* hit another sandbar, which again delayed its progress, but at 3:00 p.m. it reached the landing, where the steamer *Marquis* was anchored. On the 12th Smith ordered the *Marquis* and *Northcote* to proceed upstream. En route the *Marquis* was damaged and the *Northcote* had to tow it. The steamer arrived at Batoche again at 8:00 p.m. that evening, too late to contribute to the North-West Field Force's victory.

Major Smith concluded his formal report to Middleton by praising the zeal and coolness of his soldiers, while blaming the *Northcote*'s fate on the near-mutinous crew. "Our weakness lay in the fact that the master, pilot and engineer were aliens, and that the crew were civil employees and not enlisted men."[10] A later assessment was less circumspect: "General Middleton's navy project did little more than imperil many valuable lives and withdrew from his forces a considerable number of men who were badly needed on Saturday, Sunday and Monday."[11] This stinging condemnation perhaps does not take into account the effect the *Northcote* had in distracting the Métis and Indians from the southeast where Middleton's advance took place. The Métis channelled much energy and ammunition on the *Northcote* even after it had been incapacitated, leaving the southeast deserted and allowing Middleton to move beyond the church and rectory, which he was unable to do the following day. In fact, he would not reach that point again until the final day of fighting. The Métis had taken the *Northcote* seriously. By neutralizing one arm of Middleton's two-pronged attack, the Métis could claim an early, if short-lived, victory.

With the *Northcote* no longer a factor, the Métis regrouped to face the land attack. By this time they had formed two scout detachments, one under Patrice Fleury and another under Ambroise Champagne. Champagne patrolled the east side of the river while Fleury commanded the scouts on the west. The Métis scouts were organized in small units. Nine or ten deputy captains had been chosen, each responsible for a troop of ten men and each responsible to Gabriel Dumont.[12] On the first day of the battle the Métis scouts and riflemen were outnumbered approximately four to one.

36 Patrice Fleury, one of Riel's captains on the west side of the Saskatchewan River, *circa* 1925. (University of Saskatchewan, Saskatoon, Shortt Library of Canadiana, Morton Collection, MSS C550/2/6 [no. 1].)

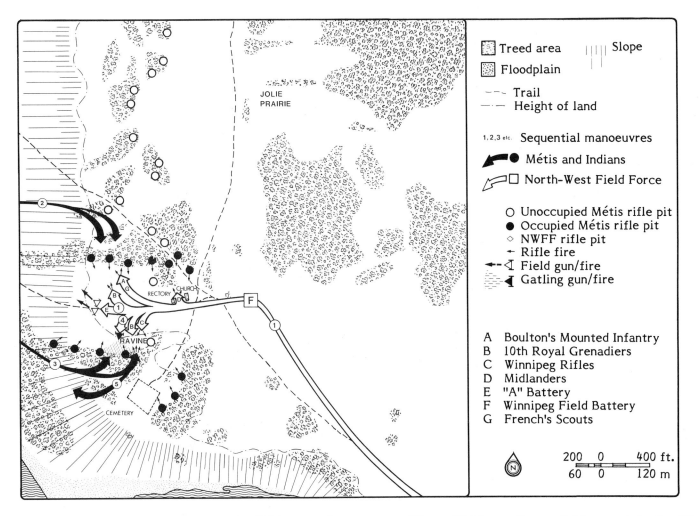

37 Day 1, 9 May, 9:00 a.m. When the Métis were drawn to the riverbank, Middleton's column was able to move past the church and rectory to Mission Ridge. As the Métis returned to their rifle pits, resistance to Middleton's advance became stiffer. Middleton threw all his men into the "firefight" to assess Métis and Indian strength. (Map by B. Richard and D. Kappler.)

As Middleton's column advanced to contact, at about 9:00 a.m., it met sporadic rifle fire from two houses along the eastern branch of the Humboldt Trail, likely the houses of Jean Caron Senior and Ludger Gareau. The two houses, hastily barricaded, stood about 400 yards from the church and rectory.[1] The first house was fired on by the Gatling gun, making the men in and around both buildings scatter. A gun from "A" Battery shelled the second house. "Some rebels immediately ran out of a ravine behind the house into the bush. The two houses took fire and were soon in ashes."[2]

Fourmond was watching the soldiers approach.

We see the red coats forming the line of battle all around the mission; using the hilly ground to hide their advance. Sensing the danger, we went in. What should we do? Put up a white flag, says Nanin. It's the Riel flag; more reason to attract shots. Seeing them still advancing, finger on the trigger, we had to decide what to do. Let's go out, said Father Fourmond, they will recognize us, and will not shoot us. We could see them perfectly, they were about 250 yds. away. We chose to go out. The cross on the church showed the temple of J.C., and indicated the priest's house and not Riel's fort. Cross put up only 3 days before. Fathers Fourmond and Végreville go out and lean on the gable wall of the house, facing the soldiers so that they could be recognized. Wearing cassocks. Barely there, a shot rings out and a bullet lands above our heads in the panelling of the house. A splinter flies in the face. It's serious, I said to [my] colleague who seemed to neither see nor hear. Let's go in, there's danger. [We are] barely in, the people are struck by fear as we hear the machine gun riddle the roof of the house.[3]

Within 100 yards of the church two rounds had been fired from the Gatling gun. According to Boulton, only the corner of the rectory had been struck by the bullets, but unknown to

38 Father Moulin, O.M.I., who was accidently shot through the leg while in the rectory during the fighting. Photo *circa* 1885. (Public Archives Canada, C-28538.)

40 Middleton at the rectory, 9 May. (Glenbow Archives, Calgary, NA-363-52.)

39 Father Vital Fourmond, O.M.I., was in the rectory for much of the fighting and later gave evidence that helped to fill in gaps in the military actions from the Métis perspective. Of the four priests at Batoche, he was the most sympathetic to the Métis. Photo *circa* 1885. (Provincial Archives of Alberta, OB 2960.)

the soldiers, Father Moulin had been hit in the leg by an errant bullet that had gone through the rectory wall. (Bullet marks can still be seen in the woodwork.) Immediately after the burst of fire a white flag or handkerchief was seen, and Middleton, who had given "strict instructions to the force to spare non-combatants as far as possible,"[4] ordered the firing stopped. A priest was waving the flag from the opened door of the rectory.[5] "Father Moulin took a piece of cotton given by the Sisters and opens the door slightly and waves it in front of the soldiers advancing in line of battle. At the same time we heard them cry: 'Don't fear! Don't fear!' "[6] Middleton approached the rectory.

I ... rode up to the house which I found to be full of people; three or four Roman Catholic priests, some sisters of mercy and a number of women and children, the latter being all half-breeds. They were naturally alarmed, and having reassured them we continued our advance.[7]

Fourmond's observations of Middleton at the time suggest that the general was in an agitated state.

Open the door and go out to meet the arriving troops, the general and his staff in front. We salute each other, the first to approach me is a friend from Prince Albert, Mr. Reid ... in Middleton's army. He introduces the general, who greets us respectfully. Introduces the officers. Then shows a newspaper; he announces laughingly to Father Fourmond: "Here is the announcement of Father Fourmond's death, is it you? It's strange, I should have been the first to know about this." It wasn't the time for jokes. The general seems very worried, looking right and left for the enemy who were not revealing their presence anywhere. Strange way to make war. He arrives at the mouth of the Métis guns without knowing where they are. We tell him: Beware, you are at Batoche, you are expected on all sides; these words are scarcely said when he gives his orders, makes his soldiers take cover from surprise attack in the ravine separating us from the cemetery. He sends the artillery forward escorted by a squadron of infantry. Fingers on the triggers of their rifles. Barely 100 yards farther, the artillery positioned at the edge of the plateau [Mission] Ridge on the trail to Batoche, [he] turns and gives the battle signal. The infantrymen fire into surrounding bushes. The Métis respond. The battle begins in earnest.[8]

It was Boulton's infantry who had advanced past the church. Now Middleton was throwing virtually his entire contingent into an all-out attack, a "firefight."[9] It was just before 9:45 a.m. Only a short distance past the church Boulton's infantry were fired upon from "a sort of low brush about 200 yards or 300 yards ahead."[10] Two companies of the 10th Royal Grenadiers were ordered to advance in skirmishing order and reached the edge of the ravine on the left. Another two companies of grenadiers moved forward on the right near the church. "A" Battery was then ordered forward to the crest of the hill — "Mission Ridge" — overlooking Batoche with both its nine-pounders and the Gatling. The field guns began to shell the houses at Batoche while the Gatling was directed at the western bank, across the river, "from where a galling fire was being kept up by a totally invisible enemy."[11] This was the most advanced position that the Field Force was able to hold that day, and it was not until the 12th that they again reached Mission Ridge.

The grenadiers and "A" Battery now came under a shower of bullets, and Boulton's Mounted Infantry "had now received a decided check. Immediately in our front lay thick bush, beyond which we could not penetrate."[12] The Gatling was ordered in to support the grenadiers and the battery. The grenadiers turned to counter the heavy fire from the left, where "desperate efforts were made to turn our left flank by their men in the bush under the high river bank and on the slope, who fired with great vigour."[13]

When Middleton himself reached Mission Ridge, he saw that "the gun detachments and horses were suffering,"[14] and ordered them to pull back. As the grenadiers near the ravine, who had been ordered to fire from lying positions, stood up to retreat, they drew even more Métis fire. The Métis seemed to be trying to cut the grenadiers off from any easterly movement. It was now that by all accounts the Gatling made its most memorable contribution by holding off enemy fire until the grenadiers could pull back in an orderly manner.

A body of enemy, who crept through the bushes which lay a short distance in our front, poured in a volley and wounded two or three men and killed a horse. The gatling, which was being worked for a second time and was just getting into action, with Captain Howard at the crank, turned its fire on the concealed foe, and for a moment silenced them. Captain Howard on this occasion showed his gun off to the best advantage, and pluckily worked it with great coolness, although the fire from the enemy was very hot for a time.[15]

Although Métis fire was intense, no one was killed. The Field Force now occupied a position just back from the crest of Mission Ridge. The Métis, firing from both bush and rifle pits, held two positions: one immediately to the right centre and the other to the left, on the heavily wooded crest of the riverbank.

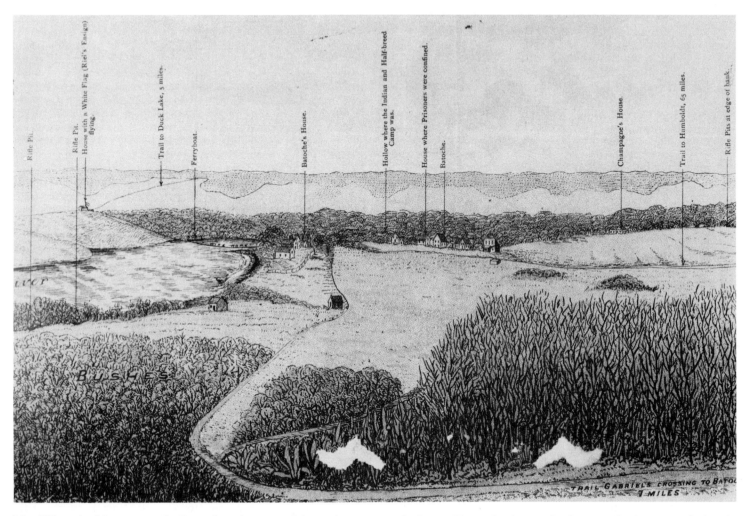

Rifle Pit.

Rifle Pit.
House with a White Flag (Riel's Ensign) flying.

Trail to Duck Lake, 5 miles.

Ferryboat.

Batoche's House.

Hollow where the Indian and Half-breed Camp was.

House where Prisoners were confined.

Batoche.

Champagne's House.

Trail to Humboldt, 65 miles.

Rifle Pits at edge of bank.

BUSHES

RIVER

TRAIL GABRIEL'S CROSSING TO BATOCHE 3 MILES

41 "View looking towards Batoche, from position whence Guns fired on 9th May, 1885." The sketch, by Captain Haig, Royal Engineers, while inaccurate for many landscape features, does show what was significant from the military point of view. Note the heavy bushes at the bottom of the slope near the church. (Canada. Parliament. House of Commons, *Sessional Papers*, Vol. 19, No. 5 [1886], p. 27.)

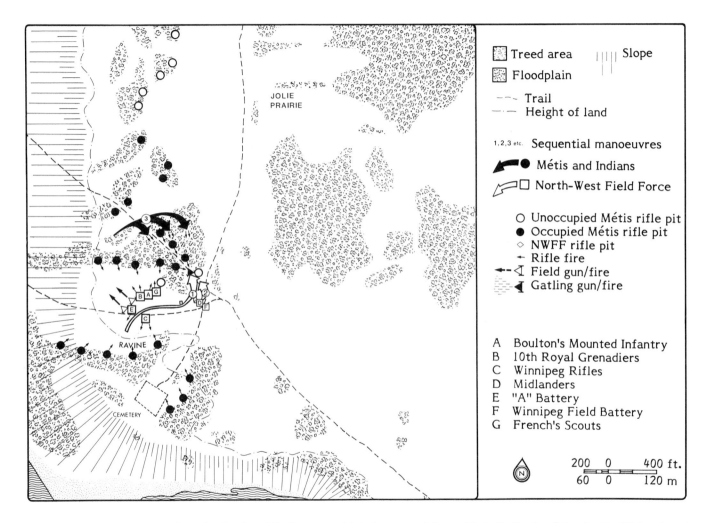

42 Day 1, 9 May, 11:00 a.m. After being checked at Mission Ridge, Middleton tried to break through the Métis lines close to the church and rectory with the help of the Gatling gun, which he moved from his left flank. (Map by B. Richard and D. Kappler.)

Legend:

- Treed area
- Floodplain
- ||| Slope
- --- Trail
- —·— Height of land
- 1,2,3 etc. Sequential manoeuvres
- Métis and Indians
- North-West Field Force
- O Unoccupied Métis rifle pit
- ● Occupied Métis rifle pit
- ◇ NWFF rifle pit
- ← Rifle fire
- ◄ Field gun/fire
- ◄ Gatling gun/fire

A Boulton's Mounted Infantry
B 10th Royal Grenadiers
C Winnipeg Rifles
D Midlanders
E "A" Battery
F Winnipeg Field Battery
G French's Scouts

JOLIE PRAIRIE
RAVINE
CEMETERY

N

200   0   400 ft.
60   0   120 m

The Gatling gun was now moved from the left flank toward the lines extending from the church. This could be considered the Field Force's second attempt to break through the Métis lines. Middleton "brought the gatling round the church and Captain Howard made a dashing attempt to flank the bluff, but could not succeed, as the enemy was ensconced in well made rifle pits."[16] The time was now about 11:00 a.m. The Winnipeg Rifles occupied the left flank along the river near the cemetery, the artillery of "A" Battery lined Mission Ridge, all companies of the grenadiers were now to the front and centre, while Boulton's Mounted Infantry and French's Scouts completed the line up to the rectory. The Midlanders and the Winnipeg Field Battery stood in reserve by the church, where Middleton watched the action.

To Lord Melgund the action was much like the fighting at Fish Creek. The soldiers of the Field Force were firing from lying positions at a well-concealed enemy,[17] and when they did fire it may well have been on the decoys that the Métis raised from their pits:

> during the battle of Batoche, during the four days, a few Métis soldiers lay flat on their stomachs behind the leafless bushes, hung their hats on the branches 3-1/2 or 4 feet high and the soldiers shot at them and the Métis, lying flat on their stomachs, watched them under the smoke and shot them almost on target.[18]

9 MAY: THE MÉTIS OFFENSIVE

The Métis made two attempts to encircle the Field Force during the first day. Their first move, made on the force's left flank, took place about 10:00 a.m., when the Gatling had had to cover the grenadiers as they pulled back from the ridge. The Métis pressure was an attempt to capture the Gatling. It was described by Elie Dumont.

We prepare to stop the soldiers from descending [from] the plateau. Suddenly we see them closer to the Church on the butte: we charged on that side, thinking they wanted to go down by that trail. I was with Philippe and Bap[tiste] Boucher, 3 in front. Others on each side a little behind. Straight ahead the gatling gun was ready, we were then among the small poplars. Philippe 2 steps in front of me and Boucher beside me. Suddenly Philippe says: "There are police on the little hill." Philippe fires and Bap[tiste] Boucher also. Men at the gatling gun started to turn it. When the gun cracked we threw ourselves down. The gatling fires at us. When the shooting ended, I ran back on the same road and my partners went on to the riverbank. Some of our people were there and wanted to go to the riverbank.... There were about 30 of us. We followed the River, avoiding open areas, to go upriver to opposite the gatling; spent an hour there fighting. Wanted to have enough people to take the gatling gun on the hill in front of us, 5 or 6 wanted to go with me. In the ravine there were about 100 people (Indians, Sioux, Cree, Métis). I planned go closer in the poplars, advance about 250 yds, 7 or 8 together, 3 Métis and Cree, there is still 100 yds to go to get the gatling: but there are not enough people.... We were grazed by bullets [as they crossed the Métis line of fire]. We stayed there about 1/2 hour, and returned on the same trail, running fast to the riverbank ... once at the river we climbed toward the cemetery, we were about 30. We got close to the cemetery. Soldiers already re-treated. They already were too far away for us to fire.[1]

After his first line of skirmishers ran into resistance and pulled back a short distance, Middleton ordered the two nine-pounders of "A" Battery forward again, and directed their fire to the western riverbank. Métis gunfire was not particularly intense at the time, and an almost unimpeded shelling by the nine-pound guns continued. Amid the shelling it was difficult for the Métis to move about and fire accurately. During the lull in Métis fire Middleton had ordered one gun further forward. Unfortunately for the general, the Métis rifle pits along the entire front were becoming fully manned as the men returned from pursuing the *Northcote*. And the gun misfired.

With a startling suddenness of a thunderbolt from a cloudless sky, a crashing fusillade ... swept through the wooded slope at the right front ... the bushy slope, which hitherto appeared to be perfectly deserted, appeared suddenly to be infested by coyotting savages. The guttural 'ki-yi-ki-yi,' the sweeping fusillade, and above everything, the startling suddenness of the eruption [of the gun], combined to make the new situation a trying one for the nerves of the bravest.[2]

Middleton ordered a retreat.

At approximately noon, after Captain Howard's attempt to outflank the Métis on the right, near the church, had failed, Middleton moved back to the left flank where he had left Melgund in command. When he arrived he found that Captain Peters "had made a gallant and vigorous attempt, with a few of the garrison artillery, to drive the enemy out of the bluff below, but had failed and had retired, leaving a wounded man [Gunner Philips] behind."[3] Then, in another attempt to clear the Métis positions below Mission Ridge, Middleton ordered the two companies of Midlanders forward, but they were not able to advance even as far as Peters's small group had gone and soon pulled back to the ridge.

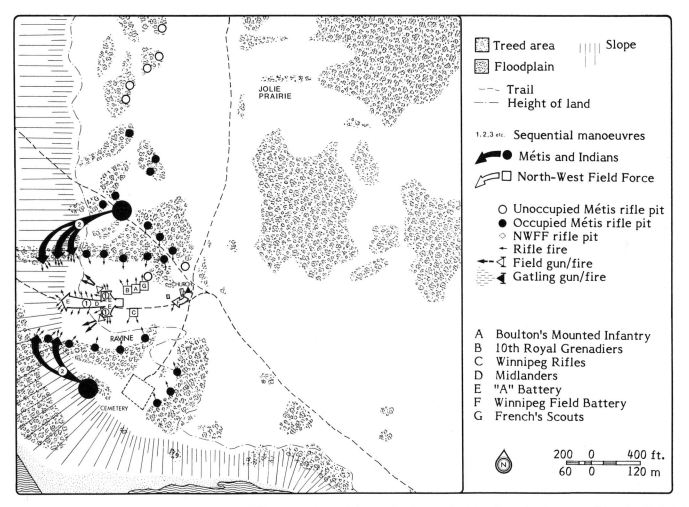

43 Day 1, 9 May, 2:00 p.m. Gunner Philips was shot when "A" Battery rushed down Mission Ridge to drive the Métis out of their pits. The rush failed and the recovery of Philips's body was led by Captain Peters. (Map by B. Richard and D. Kappler.)

Legend content:

Treed area
Floodplain
Slope
Trail
Height of land

1, 2, 3 etc. Sequential manoeuvres
Métis and Indians
North-West Field Force

○ Unoccupied Métis rifle pit
● Occupied Métis rifle pit
◇ NWFF rifle pit
← Rifle fire
◄─ Field gun/fire
◄ Gatling gun/fire

A Boulton's Mounted Infantry
B 10th Royal Grenadiers
C Winnipeg Rifles
D Midlanders
E "A" Battery
F Winnipeg Field Battery
G French's Scouts

JOLIE PRAIRIE
CHURCH
RAVINE
CEMETERY

200 0 400 ft.
60 0 120 m

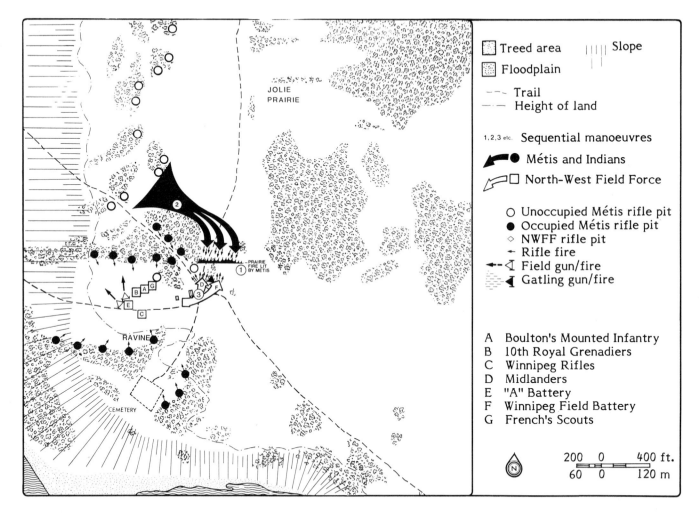

Treed area | Slope
Floodplain
--- Trail
—·— Height of land

1,2,3 etc. Sequential manoeuvres

Métis and Indians
North-West Field Force

○ Unoccupied Métis rifle pit
● Occupied Métis rifle pit
◇ NWFF rifle pit
← Rifle fire
◄─◁ Field gun/fire
◀ Gatling gun/fire

A Boulton's Mounted Infantry
B 10th Royal Grenadiers
C Winnipeg Rifles
D Midlanders
E "A" Battery
F Winnipeg Field Battery
G French's Scouts

JOLIE PRAIRIE

PRAIRIE FIRE LIT BY MÉTIS

RAVINE

CEMETERY

200 0 400 ft.
60 0 120 m

44 Day 1, 9 May, 3:00 p.m. The Métis attempted to pinch off Middleton's column from its supplies, trying to advance under a smoke screen. With the aid of the Gatling gun the Field Force withstood the offensive. (Map by B. Richard and D. Kappler.)

51

Around 2:00 p.m. Peters organized an attempt to rescue Philips for some thought Philips had only been wounded. One man had heard him crying out: "Captain French, my leg is broken. For God's sake, don't leave me here." When they reached him, he was dead.[4]

After Philips's body was recovered, the Métis made a second attempt to encircle the Field Force, this time from the north. The Métis took advantage of the northwesterly wind blowing toward the church. They lit a prairie fire upwind and fired under the cover of the smoke, a manoeuvre that threatened to cut Middleton's supply line to the east.[5] This unanticipated tactic ruffled some of the senior officers. Melgund described its effects:

> things looking awkward we got wounded out of church [set up as a temporary hospital] into waggons, and had ordered them to fall back to camp. I found that the ammunition waggons were also retiring, and I stopped them, much to Disprowe's relief, who was in charge of them, and had done well all day.[6]

But although the fire briefly caused some anxiety for the right flank, it apparently burned out and was not followed by any sustained Métis advance.

The Métis attempt to pinch off the Field Force from their supplies had been withstood, and the heavy fire from both sides subsided, "though a head shown by either party was a target for a score of bullets."[7] It was now 3:00 p.m. Middleton decided to send his chief of staff, Lord Melgund, to the telegraph station at Humboldt, ostensibly to send a private message to Caron. The real purpose of the mission remains clouded with controversy. Later innuendo in the eastern press hinted that Middleton had lost his composure and anticipated a lengthy battle that he feared his column might lose. Yet, after a difficult day in the field, the general might -- as he himself stated -- simply have sent Melgund to organize another column in case his first attempt to take Batoche was thwarted.

The order to send Melgund to Humboldt was apparently linked to Middleton's more general concern over the effect that withdrawing his troops would have on his men and on the Métis. Even a small withdrawal from the front could heighten enemy morale. Middleton had a choice: either he could go back seven miles to the previous night's camp, or he could move the camp closer to the front, perhaps placing his force in danger of encirclement.

> It was getting late, and I saw that, though we were holding our own, it would not be advisable to risk an attempt to advance through the thick cover which surrounded the village, which was now swarming with the enemy, reinforced by the party who had been engaged attacking the steamer, and I had to decide as to where we should camp for the night. Most, if not all of my senior officers were of the opinion that we were not strong enough and ought to retire to our last camp and await reinforcements. I differed from them. I considered, though I would have been glad of a few more men, that we were strong enough as we were, and a few days delay before actually forcing the enemy's position would duly render our men more fit and anxious for it, and we could afford to expend more ammunition than the enemy. Moreover, even if reinforcements were found to be necessary, we could await them more advantageously where we were for I felt certain that should we retire, we should be followed up, and our retirement might chance to become a rout. Even if we fell back unmolested, the fact of our retiring at all would be made the most of all over the territories, and a general rising would probably take place. So I determined to hold on at all hazards where we were, even to keeping with us the wounded, whom I at one time thought of sending back. At the same time, I thought it wise to prepare for possibilities and wrote orders to be sent by telegraph from Humboldt to close up the troops on our line of communication, so as to be at hand if required.[8]

Not everyone agreed with the general's version of this moment. Dr. Orton, the brigade surgeon, wrote another account, published in the *Toronto Daily Mail* on 29 January 1886. Orton also wrote to Caron to correct what he thought were inaccuracies in the official accounts of the fighting published in the *Sessional Papers* of parliament in 1886. Orton emphasized what he viewed as Middleton's indecision, hesitancy and, particularly, his lack of initiative. He de-

GRENADIERS ON PICKET FISH CREEK
A LULL IN THE FIGHT
GETTING THROUGH THE GRAVEYARD
90TH VICTORY! 10 9
DINNER UNDER DIFFICULTIES
THE W.F.B. WAITING FOR ORDERS
WORKING THE GATLING

clared that Middleton continually underestimated and denigrated the fighting capacity of his Canadian men and officers. Orton claimed, furthermore, that Middleton had ordered the men back to the previous night's camp, and that it was he, Orton, who prevailed on the general to cancel his orders to withdraw.

In an exchange of correspondence between Melgund and Middleton during the winter of 1886, Middleton expressed concern over the defamations of "the drunken Doctor Orton." It appears that Middleton hoped Melgund would publish a response to Orton's letter in the *Mail* and vindicate the official government account Middleton had written. Melgund, however, had trouble complying. According to Melgund, against his advice and that of Van Straubenzie, Middleton "finally decided to camp where he was, a very dangerous place, but no doubt the effect of retiring would be very bad, and possibly the rebels seeing that he holds his own, may fall back and disperse during the night."[9] Melgund had obviously initially been under the impression that the troops would retire the seven miles to the previous night's camp:

> my opinion when we talked over what was to be done at Batoche was that it would be right to retire to our [previous] camp on the prairie and I said so to you ... but you will no doubt recollect that you had told me either the evening before or the morning of the advance on Batoche that should we be unable to go straight in you would make a reconnaissance of it and retire to your camp and that the possibility of such a movement had been considered before hand....[10]

45 "Sketches from the Front," *The Canadian Pictorial and Illustrated War News*, Vol. 1, No. 10, 6 June 1885. (Manitoba Archives.)

Melgund then offered Middleton his explanation of the cancelled orders that Orton emphasized. In Melgund's account Middleton was not as vacillating as Orton's accusations suggested. Instead, Melgund himself took responsibility for the confusion during the allegedly cancelled retreat, stating that he ordered the withdrawal of the wounded stopped since the ammunition on the wagons carrying them was still needed:

> the rebels set fire to the brush in front of the church in which were our wounded. The rebels made, (I explained they might) advances under the cover of smoke, and that [Orton's] wounded would be in danger in the church. I then per your order told Dr. Orton to get the wounded out of the church and to move off towards the camp. This was done. But soon afterwards I found that [the] ammunition waggons had gone off with the wounded. I went after them to stop [the] ammunition. My impression is that all waggons with ammunition and wounded were stopped by this rider. They had not gone far and you soon after decided to remain where you were and to make camp on the prairie.

> It seems possible that this order of mine to stop his ammunition waggons may be his foundation for his statement in the letter as to his orders for retreat being cancelled.[11]

In any case, by approximately 3:00 p.m. the fighting had subsided.[12] Middleton ordered the camp moved forward to within a mile of Batoche, about a quarter-mile from the church. Between approximately 3 and 4 p.m. Boulton's men and J.E. Secretan, the assistant transport officer, were dispatched to bring the previous night's camp forward. Three and a half hours later the transport carrying the camp arrived.

A zareba was basically a corral formed by wagons rein-
forced by supplies and anything movable, and often surrounded by earthworks or thorn bushes. Its construction depended
on the length of time an army intended to remain in a
locality and on whether attack upon the camp was anticipated. Captain Charles Callwell, a nineteenth-century military expert, stated that a zareba could be either a base camp
for an attack on the enemy or a haven for retreat especially
useful for protection at night.[1] At Batoche the zareba was
both: the base for movements out against the Métis and
Indians at the start of each day, and the place to which the
soldiers withdrew at the end of the day's fighting. It allowed
Middleton and his men a chance to regroup — especially after
their "decided check" the first day. The zareba also protected the large transport — 160 wagons, 600 horses and 80
cattle — that supported the 886-man contingent.[2]

As the site for his new camp Middleton chose high ground
close to the river with as much open space surrounding it as
possible and with the natural defence of the river to the
south. The area might have been more dangerous as a
bivouac later in the season, but the scattered poplar copses in
the immediate vicinity were as yet without leaves and did not
afford substantial cover to the Métis and Indians.

The zareba was located in a "ploughed field," the property
of Jean Caron Senior.[3] Captain Haig, a Royal Engineer, was
sent to choose the precise location of the camp:

> there was only one place where it was open enough for
> a camp, and that within 150 yards of the woods. It
> was a ploughed field which fortunately included two
> ponds. I took two artillery horses, harnessed them in a
> plough, and ran two furrows round to work the outline
> of what was to be our camp, or rather bivouac.[4]

Haig faced the everpresent danger that "the Indians might
work around our right flank and cut us off from our wagons
which contained food and supplies."[5]

46 Captain H. de H. Haig of the Royal Engineers, a regular
British officer on Middleton's staff, *circa* 1880s. (Courtesy
Jack Summers.)

47 View from the site of the Field Force pickets on the riverbank south of the zareba. (Photo by B. Lobchuk.)

One soldier remembered that it was in a ploughed field on rising ground.[6] R.C. Laurie of the Winnipeg Rifles wrote that it was built "on bald prairie."[7] It enclosed a little slough, "thus assuring a supply of water."[8] One of French's Scouts wrote that it was built "of all horrors in a ploughed field surrounded by bluffs and on the left a deep ravine."[9] Major Boulton said that it was a quarter-mile from the church and 200 yards from the riverbank and that the houses close by were burnt down as a precautionary measure.[10] Another soldier remembered that the transport arrived to form a "corral enclosing about 12 acres with wagons on all sides."[11] Arthur Wheeler with the Dominion Land Surveyors stated that "according to theory it was on high ground."[12]

The zareba was in the most advantageous position possible for the North-West Field Force. It was on the highest ground possible, close to the enemy, in as open an area as could be

48 Outside the zareba. (Public Archives Canada, C-3454.)

49 Soldiers resting inside the zareba. Judging by their equipment, the men are officers of one of the infantry units engaged at Batoche. (Public Archives Canada, C-4522.)

found, and in a location that took advantage of the natural defences afforded by the steep riverbank. The Métis and Indians were consequently left with few areas on which they could advance without being seen. The view from the riverbank allowed the pickets of the Field Force to observe any use that might have been made of the river or its banks (their pickets did not occupy this high point until the evening of the 10th). The open ground immediately to the north and west would have exposed any daytime advance from these directions.

Construction of the zareba began in mid- to late afternoon. "The Royals proved they had lost none of their former skill in field engineering. After a hard day's marching and fighting, they were put to work entrenching the bivouac area, throwing up earthworks, and arranging wagons for defence."[13] The men worked with anything at their disposal, "digging with bayonets, swords and scooping with tin plates."[14] Haig "had got a few of the men ... to make a tiny parapet of plough sods and fence rails on the dangerous side of the bivouac, and as wagons came up they were laagered inside this."[15]

The breastworks were made of almost anything the soldiers could lay their hands on: "fence rails, bags of oats, bales of hay...."[16]

> Entrenchment in which troops were placed was made by throwing up sods about four or five feet high, and inside of this about fifteen or sixteen feet from the breastwork, a second square was made of transport wagons, placed in such a position that the tongue of one wagon was inside the next one to it, all the baggage and provisions being left in the wagons. Towards the centre of this square another earthwork was thrown up to protect the hospital tents. There were within the encampment the 90th [Winnipeg Rifles], the 10th Royals, the Midland Battalion, and four nine pounders, besides horses, mules, cayuses, and horned beasts of all ages, and lastly an instrument known as "Captain Howard's hurdy-gurdy"....[17]

The most vulnerable areas of the zareba were its northwestern, northern and eastern sides. In the west to northwest, where the zareba was particularly low and, as Haig

stated, could not be protected,[18] three rows of wagons were drawn up. Considered especially vulnerable was the northern side — where, 100 yards from the zareba, the bushes and undulating terrain of another slough might have provided cover for an attack — so in that area additional earthworks were angled northward outside the zareba and all four nine-pounders were placed at angles in openings in the earthworks to allow a wide and flexible range of fire, but one that could be concentrated on the north and east. No attack came from the north, no encircling movements were attempted, and no prairie fire, like the one the Métis had set that afternoon, threatened the camp. Nevertheless, these flanks were the most exposed and potentially the most vulnerable.

Outside the zareba along its western flank two lines of rifle pits, constructed by the 10th, along with the zareba wall, gave Middleton a triple line of defence against attack from the direction of the cemetery. A line of rifle pits on the southern flank of the zareba covered the riverbank, where the bush was closest and where the Field Force did receive some harassing fire on the evenings of the 9th and 10th, but never were these defences seriously threatened.

At approximately 6:30 p.m. a renewed advance from the Métis coincided with the gradual withdrawal of the troops to the zareba, "some of the enemy following them up until checked by a heavy fire from the zareba."[19] The Gatling gun was again relied upon to cover a retreat. "The rebels, well aware of our retirement, took advantage of their safe route under the brow of the cliff, and rising over the brow fired into the zareba."[20] Both the Winnipeg Rifles and the 10th Royal Grenadiers were deployed to meet the Métis pursuit. "The wonder is that our loss was not heavy. The only reasonable explanations are poor ammunition, poor and hurried marksmanship, greater caution on the part of our forces, and a kind Providence."[21]

The Métis and Indians seemed to think the Field Force was defeated and "came down on the zareba." During this difficult time when the Métis poured a heavy fire into the camp, the soldiers "scrambled for something to eat."[22] On completing a meal of hardtack and tea brewed from the alkaline slough water (the only way it could be drunk), companies were detailed to building up the defences: "all

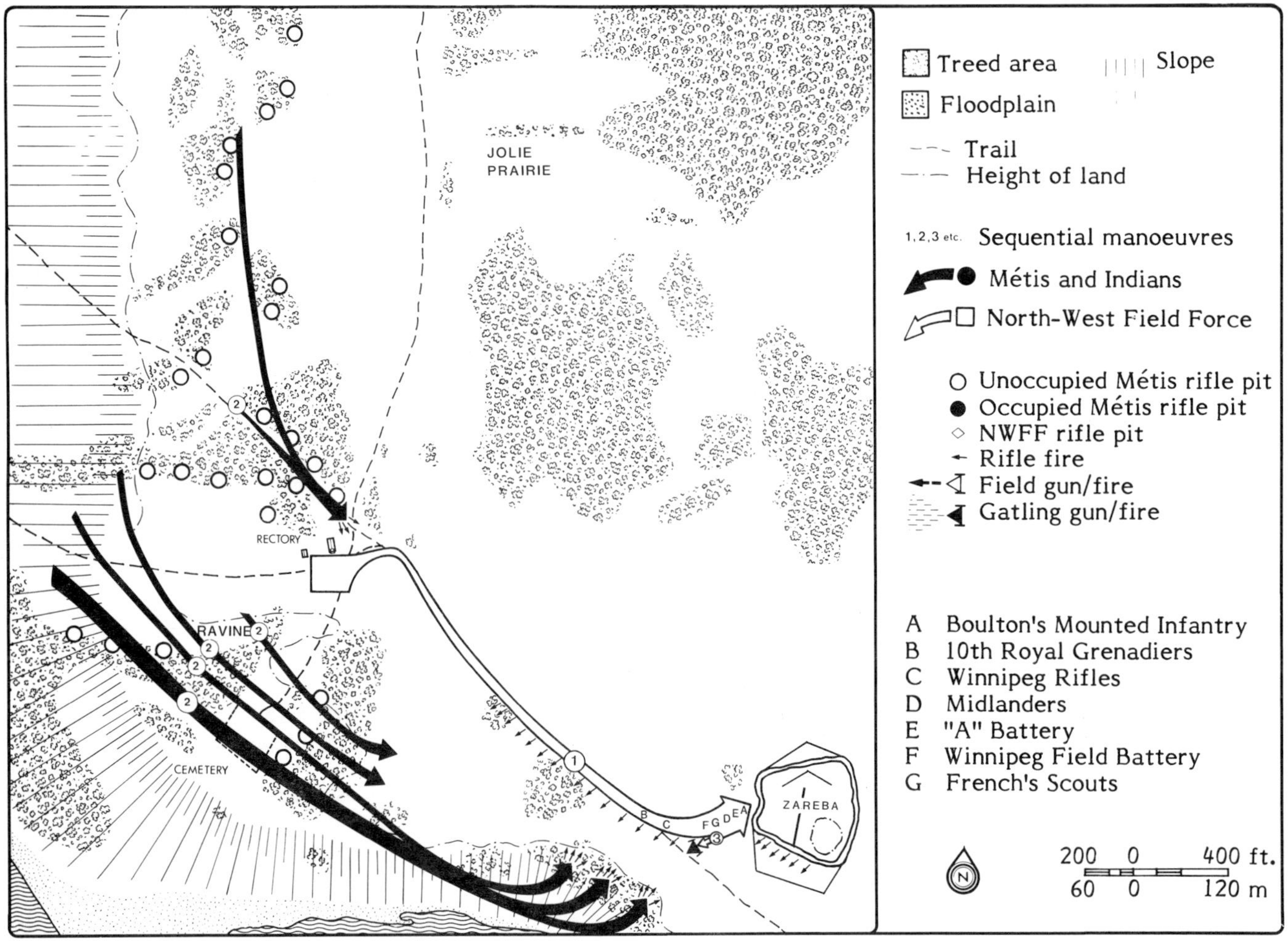
JOLIE
PRAIRIE
RECTORY
RAVINE
CEMETERY
ZAREBA
Treed area
Slope
Floodplain
Trail
Height of land
1,2,3 etc. Sequential manoeuvres
Métis and Indians
North-West Field Force
Unoccupied Métis rifle pit
Occupied Métis rifle pit
NWFF rifle pit
Rifle fire
Field gun/fire
Gatling gun/fire
A Boulton's Mounted Infantry
B 10th Royal Grenadiers
C Winnipeg Rifles
D Midlanders
E "A" Battery
F Winnipeg Field Battery
G French's Scouts
200 0 400 ft.
60 0 120 m

50 Day 1, 9 May, 6:00 p.m. During the soldiers' withdrawal into the zareba the Métis and Indians harassed them from the cover of the bush along the riverbank. (Map by B. Richard and D. Kappler.)

hands turned to making trenches outside the wagons ... as close as could be got extending right around the zareba, all hands at work on this for some hours until breastworks thrown up all around the zareba and a trench to lie in."[23]

At dusk, around 7:00 p.m., the fire lessened to intermittent, long-range shooting. As the fighting waned, the men prepared for the night. Only the wounded were allowed to sleep in tents; the rest had to make do under the open sky.

Night came at length, but tired as we were it was scarcely welcome. We were cooped up, and had the extreme satisfaction of furnishing a good mark for pot shooters.... Men were busy throwing up hasty entrenchments; teamsters, nervous and frightened, were yelling at equally nervous animals; around the hospital tents the doctors were busy in dressing wounds, probing for bullets, etc. The bullets were whizzing and pinging overhead, and occasionally striking inside. Pleasant prospect for the night, especially when one remembered that a favorite trick among the reds is to stampede the cattle and horses of the enemy. Hoofs would be apt to deal worse wounds than balls, and against affrighted animals, cooped up within a small space, we had absolutely no defence. The anticipations of a mean night were largely realized, though thus far we have escaped a stampede. Few, if any, slept five hours consecutively, and the firing was kept up almost all night.[24]

By 10 o'clock "a fairly presentable earthworks" had been thrown up.[25] Some of the men were in the trenches. An officer had been put in charge of each side of the zareba and sentinels posted. The Midlanders and a company of the Winnipeg Rifles were on picket duty on the riverbank, "occasionally searching the wooded banks with a volley."[26] The men, their guns loaded beside them, tried to sleep. Gunfire peppered the camp all night, "but beyond shooting a couple of horses, and the wounding of two Grenadiers ... no damage was done."[27]

By the end of the first day of fighting at Batoche, Middleton and the North-West Field Force were in an enclosed encampment, men and animals spending a fretful night huddled in the zareba. By contrast the Métis and Indians were in an almost victorious mood. As Fourmond observed, "it seemed the army was running away. And victory won by the Métis, who were chasing the enemy, but staying beyond the range of the gatling gun."[28] They kept up a disconcerting fire into the zareba throughout the night, the Indians doing much of the shooting.

A big gang sat down. We drew plans for the evening. Indians saying we should fight them tonight in their camp; all night: you Métis can work in the day. Métis say yes. As dusk fell, Indians began firing on the camp, about 10 minutes between shots, all night until daybreak.[29]

The priests who occupied the church took "advantage of the free time after the soldiers retreated to go out and take a breath of fresh air and hear the news."[30] On the first day they noted that the Field Force appeared ill-prepared and disorganized,[31] but they also noted the shortage of ammunition among the Métis: "we would see Sioux, prowling in the field the soldiers had left, [looking for] abandoned or lost cartridges, stocking up for the next day."[32] When a shell did not explode, it too had been used for ammunition: "Michel Trottier's son picks up the shell, goes down the hill with the powder it contains and picks up soldiers' bullets, and takes them to be melted down to make bullets for the Métis."[33]

The priests also sensed that the Métis may have gained a false sense of security from the method of firing the Field Force used: "the Métis are often misled as to the number of soldiers killed because of the routine that the first row drops down while the second fires."[34] The recognition by the Métis that they were killing fewer men than they had believed may have diminished their enthusiasm after the apparent victory of the 9th.

Métis and Indian resistance on the first day appears to have stunned Middleton momentarily. His decision to move the camp up to the front showed that he still had confidence in his men's ability to break through the defences at Batoche, yet his actions during the next few days were cautious and deliberate. Even though his intelligence reports were showing the Métis fewer in number than he had estimated and low on ammunition, Middleton was unwilling to embark on a bold offensive[35] even though he had lost only two men and a few wounded. His caution was demonstrated on the evening of the 9th when he again sent a messenger to telegraph for more troops. He could still not be certain about the strength of the Métis nor could he know what reinforcements his enemy might call upon. In effect, he was imposing a partial siege on Batoche.

"A heavy dew had fallen during the night, but a more charming morning than the 10th of May never dawned."[1] Perhaps it was the Sabbath that stayed a major offensive by either side that day. The soldiers rose before dawn to be prepared should the Métis attack at first light, but their fears proved unfounded. "A hurried breakfast was made of hardtack, bacon, and tea, and then a brief delay occurred, the General waiting to hear from the scouts who had gone forward to the outskirts of the bush."[2] The day began quietly with the soldiers moving out of the camp toward the lines held on the previous day. At a point approximately halfway between the zareba and the cemetery, well ahead of the row of rifle pits dug on the 9th, they dug a line of shallow pits in a half-moon across the road. They were unable to reach Mission Ridge "as the enemy was in greater force, and now held the high ground about the cemetery and the ground in front of the church. Some of them, apparently Indians from their war cries, had taken post at the end of the point of land below the cemetery."[3]

The Midlanders had not been moved up to the front but were detailed to improve the rifle pits on the southern flank.

With pick-axes and shovels we began our work but were not allowed to proceed unmolested as we would frequently receive a heavy volley from the front and sometimes from the right flank which rendered it necessary for us to abandon for a time our implements and resort to our firearms; when we would drop down behind our half constructed entrenchments and direct a heavy fire against the desperate and defiant rebels. It continued this way until we had our rifle pit completed, fortunately no one was wounded during our operations. The teamsters, who numbered 200 lost no time in rendering the zareba well nigh impregnable as they were chiefly engaged during the day throwing up formidable earthworks so in case of our being driven to extremity the whole force could occupy and retain it against the whole rebel force.[4]

Haig, again in charge of reinforcing the zareba, was still concerned about the low ground to the northwest. Efforts were therefore directed to ensure that bullets from that area could not wreak havoc on men on the higher ground inside the camp. Already three rows of wagons stood there to protect the vulnerable front, but more elaborate defences were needed. "We cut down bushes, strengthened our parapets, putting up three large mounds (parados) to protect the camp from the enemy's fire."[5] Two parados were built in a V-shape at the north end; another ran just off centre down the spine of the zareba. The parados were reported to be four to five feet high.[6] (No physical remains of the parados are evident today; the zareba's southern flank and interior features were probably levelled by Jean Caron when he resumed cultivating the field after the battle. The other sides have remained undisturbed for they, in fact, marked the limits of Caron's field on the north, east and west.)

Middleton's plan for the day was to demoralize the enemy with heavy artillery fire. Shortly after 5:00 a.m. he began to fire on positions his men had held the previous day. As well, "two guns were directed against the houses in the basin-shaped depression along the river [on the opposite bank]. A few rebels lay behind three log shanties just below the river bank, and the artillery soon drove them out."[7] The tactic of using artillery to demoralize the enemy can be directly traced to a recommendation in the *Soldier's Pocketbook*, published in 1869: artillery's effect on morale "is powerful; it frightens far more than it kills."[8] Middleton later recalled that "during the day 'A' Battery had some practice at some houses on the opposite bank, and two guns of the Winnipeg Battery shelled the cemetery and some rifle pits."[9] The guns were firing from a line approximately halfway between the zareba and the cemetery.

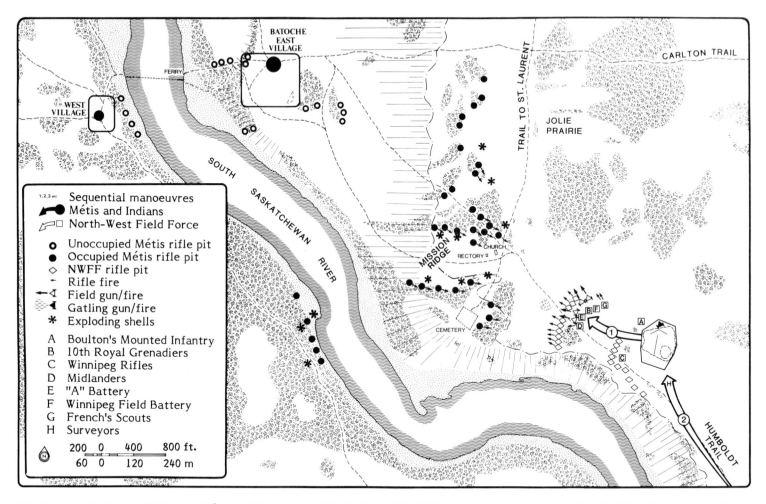

51 Day 2, 10 May. With the Métis well ensconced in their rifle pits, Middleton's men were only able to advance to a point halfway between the zareba and the cemetery. The Field Force spent most of the day shelling the west bank and the Métis rifle pits around the cemetery. (Map by B. Richard and D. Kappler.)

Legend content within map:

1,2,3 etc. Sequential manoeuvres
Métis and Indians
North-West Field Force

o Unoccupied Métis rifle pit
● Occupied Métis rifle pit
◇ NWFF rifle pit
⊢ Rifle fire
◀ Field gun/fire
◀ Gatling gun/fire
∗ Exploding shells

A Boulton's Mounted Infantry
B 10th Royal Grenadiers
C Winnipeg Rifles
D Midlanders
E "A" Battery
F Winnipeg Field Battery
G French's Scouts
H Surveyors

200 0   400   800 ft.
60   0   120   240 m

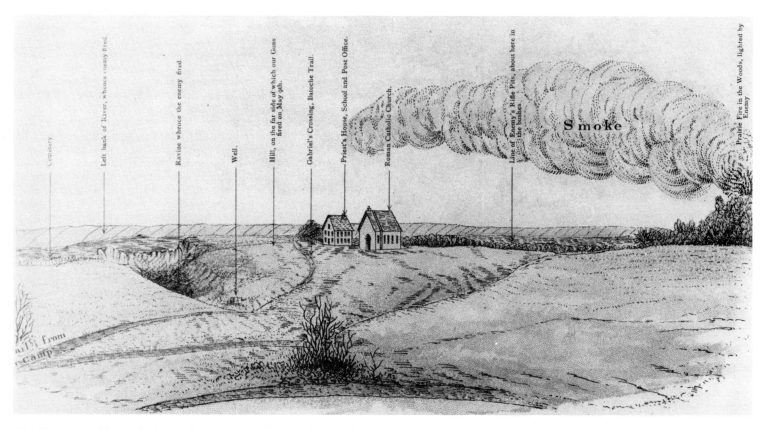

Cemetery.

Left bank of River, whence enemy fired.

Ravine whence the enemy fired.

Well.

Hill, on the far side of which our Guns fired on May 9th.

Gabriel's Crossing, Batoche Trail.

Priest's House, School and Post Office.

Roman Catholic Church.

Line of Enemy's Rifle Pits, about here in the bushes

Smoke

Prairie Fire in the Woods, lighted by the Enemy

52 "Batoche: View of the position to which we advanced on the 9th, 10th and 11th May, 1885," by Captain Haig. (Canada. Parliament. House of Commons, *Sessional Papers*, Vol. 19, No. 5 [1886], p. 26.)

Then at 8:00 a.m. Middleton had ordered the Midlanders to occupy the left flank next to the river, the 10th Royal Grenadiers having already taken up positions to the centre and right. Boulton's Mounted Infantry had been ordered out to a position just outside the camp "to protect ... the camp from surprise [from a northwesterly] direction."[10] While the infantry had been ordered to move forward as far as possible, action was generally limited to a dropping fire by the artillery. A number of opportunities for the soldiers presented themselves as a result of the success of the artillery fire, and the openings were taken advantage of; however, on each occasion the Métis thwarted the forward movement:

53 The church and rectory at Batoche, detail from "How the Royal Grenadiers got their Dinner before Batoche," *The Canadian Pictorial and Illustrated War News,* Vol. 1, No. 10, 6 June 1885. The heavily treed areas to the left centre and behind the church provided the Métis rifle pits with cover. The sketch likely depicts the fighting on the second or third days since the Field Force did not get to the church and rectory then but dug in about halfway between the church-rectory axis and the zareba. (Glenbow Archives, Calgary, NA-1480-14.)

the rebel shanties along the river were knocked into splinters by 8:30 a.m., and troops were ordered up to make a dash for the principal houses behind the bluffs. But the men had no sooner formed on the slope than the rebels on the west bank of the river popped up, and began firing, many with Winchesters at long range.

Six or seven volunteers were wounded here, and the men were at once ordered back. This was repeated two or three times during the day.[11]

Some time during the afternoon, Middleton's numbers were bolstered by the arrival of the Dominion Land Surveyors Intelligence Corps, 50 surveyors commanded by Captain J.S. Dennis, "a most useful, able body of well-mounted men, all more or less surveyors by profession."[12] Irvine of the North-West Mounted Police was ready to move south from Prince Albert toward Batoche so that the Métis and Indians would be engaged on two sides, but the manoeuvre was not ordered. At this point the general appeared content to wait.

In the afternoon Middleton ordered the half-moon line of rifle pits immediately west of the zareba to be dug deeper. These would be manned during the withdrawal of the troops at the end of the day in the hope of preventing the aggressive and dangerous pursuit by the Métis and Indians that had caused so much confusion in the retreat of the previous evening. This tactic proved to be largely successful although some damage was done, specifically to Middleton's shaving kit. "After the enemy had retired, two shots — evidently long range, unaimed shots — struck the camp, one killing a horse, the other oddly enough, striking a wagon on which was my looking glass and before which I was shaving, after which all was quiet for the night."[13] Middleton liked to portray a nonchalant attitude under fire. His description of Dumont's bullet piercing his cap at Fish Creek had a similar tone.

By 6:00 p.m. the troops had withdrawn under the heaviest fire of the day, their pursuers being kept at bay by fire from the rifle pits just west of the zareba. A prayer service led by the Reverend Mr. Gordon, who had arrived that afternoon from Winnipeg, seemed to raise the men's spirits. "During his sermon the retirement took place ... accompanied by heavy firing.... This made his remarks so much the more impressive, as he had to raise his voice above the din of firing."[14] The Métis fighters had no such support from their clergymen.

The evening of the 10th passed more quickly than that of the 9th. Middleton felt that his men were gaining the experience necessary for an all-out attack on Batoche, although to some of his men it seemed that "his aim [was] to starve the rebels out."[15]

54 Men of the Dominion Land Surveyors Intelligence Corps, a scout corps formed of surveyors working in the territories when the fighting broke out. Winchesters, ammunition and haversacks were their only equipment provided by the military. (Saskatchewan Archives Board, S-B 5767.)

Father Fourmond summarized the day's activities from the other side of the lines.

> Middleton's soldiers were sparing of their shots. They were firing only in response. We thought it pained them to profane Sunday's rest. Riel's people on the other hand seemed eager to show their ardour for the new religion, not recognizing this day's sanctity. We saw them dig holes in several places around the hillside, trying to prevent the artillery from taking the advanced positions it had held the day before. We did not get as close today as we did yesterday. We did not notice any wounded today.[16]

On the 11th, although Middleton appeared more anxious for a direct engagement with the Métis and Indians, he still behaved with caution. Most of the day was spent exploring all the possibilities available for a major attack, and the fighting escalated as a result of Middleton's reconnaissance.

Reports of open prairie just to the north of the zareba drew Middleton's interest. The area, overlooking the village of Batoche, was known by the Métis as the "Jolie Prairie." About ten o'clock, accompanied by Captain Howard with the Gatling gun and Boulton's Mounted Infantry, Middleton rode north through the swampy slough under the cover of bushes lying to the north of the zareba, emerging in an irregularly

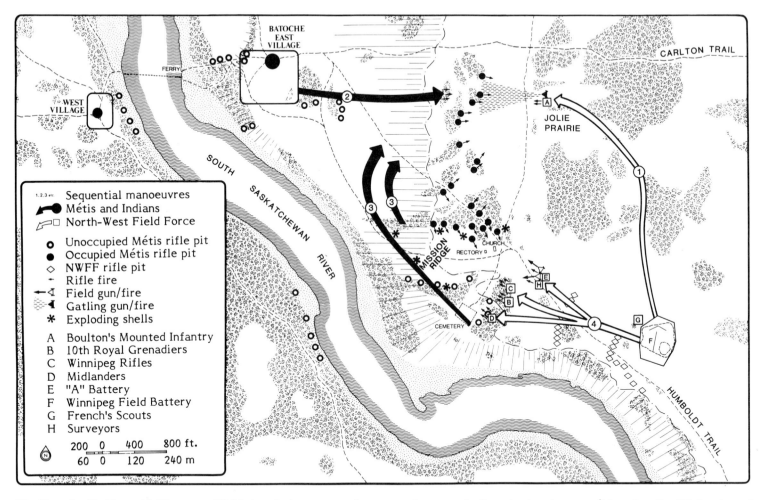

55 Day 3, 11 May, 11:00 a.m. Middleton led a reconnaissance to the Jolie Prairie. The Métis left their pits around the church and rectory and moved to the north where a brief exchange of fire took place. (Map by B. Richard and D. Kappler.)

Legend (on map):

1.2.3 etc — Sequential manoeuvres
Métis and Indians
North-West Field Force

○ Unoccupied Métis rifle pit
● Occupied Métis rifle pit
◇ NWFF rifle pit
⊣ Rifle fire
◄— Field gun/fire
◄ Gatling gun/fire
✻ Exploding shells

A Boulton's Mounted Infantry
B 10th Royal Grenadiers
C Winnipeg Rifles
D Midlanders
E "A" Battery
F Winnipeg Field Battery
G French's Scouts
H Surveyors

200 0   400   800 ft.
60   0   120   240 m

shaped plain "about two miles long and 1,000 yards in the broadest part, with a sort of slight ridge running down the centre and some undulations."[17] As they moved northward they attracted sporadic sniper fire from the rifle pits along the ridge. In response, Middleton ordered the Gatling to direct two or three rounds into the pits. Farther north the soldiers pursued but lost two men spotted riding across the prairie and captured another errant unarmed man, later discovered to be one of Riel's men, who came out of the bush. "We also captured some cattle and ponies which we took back to camp with us," and before leaving the area "burned down some log houses that might offer shelter to the enemy, in case further operations were needed here."[18]

Middleton had received intelligence reports that indicated the Métis were out of ammunition. Now he could also see that they were thinly spread out. As well, "we could see with our glasses that the enemy had a series of rifle pits all along the edge of those woods, and numbers of them were running up between the woods and disappearing into the pits. Evidently they were prepared for an attack in this direction."[19] It was clear that the Métis had responded to Middleton's manoeuvre by pulling men away from the cemetery and Mission Ridge to reinforce the northern part of their line where the Field Force "drew a smart fire."[20] He also sensed that the Métis could not be sure how many men he might deploy in a manoeuvre to the north because of the cover offered by the intervening bushes.

Further evidence that the Métis had followed the Gatling gun to the north awaited Middleton when he came back to camp. The infantry had been able to regain some of the ground they had held on the first day of fighting. "A party of

56 Philippe Chamberland, photographed <u>circa</u> 1885, a French Canadian from Bellevue (in present-day Saskatchewan), was in the rifle pits at Batoche and was sometimes the cook for the Métis councillors. (Courtesy Gérard Chamberland.)

Midlanders, under Lieutenant-Colonel William's command, finding the fire slacken from the Indians' post below the cemetery, and led by him, gallantly rushed it, the Indians bolting leaving behind them some blankets and a dummy which they had used for drawing our fire."[21] As a consequence of the infantry's advance, the artillery was again able to draw up to the vicinity of the graveyard to open fire on the houses on the opposite bank, "where we observed that the shells created great consternation among the rebels, making them scatter and get well beyond range, and silencing the long range rifles which were a constant source of annoyance."[22]

It was now clearer to Middleton than it had been in any of the previous days that the resources of the Métis and Indians were running low. Accompanying this realization was his belief that "my men were becoming more at home in this mode of warfare."[23] The plan for the last day was forming in his mind. The Métis hardly pursued the Field Force as it retired for the night and there was no gunfire into the camp that evening. Late that evening Middleton made his decision. "Our men were beginning to show more dash, and that night I came to the conclusion that it was time to make our decisive attack."[24]

12 MAY: THE FINAL DAY

The plan was straightforward and simple. Convinced that the Métis and Indians would follow his manoeuvre with the Gatling gun, Middleton would again threaten attack from the Jolie Prairie and an attack from the left flank would be led by Van Straubenzie's brigade. Van Straubenzie was to proceed to the original front by the cemetery. Then, "as soon as he heard us well engaged he was to move off, and, having taken up yesterday's position, push on towards the village."[1]

The men carrying out the feint under Middleton were Boulton's Mounted Infantry, Captain Dennis's surveyors, French's Scouts (about 150 mounted men), one gun of "A" Battery under Captain Drury, and the Gatling under Lieutenant Rivers accompanied by Captain Howard.[2] On reaching the Jolie Prairie the nine-pounder was pulled up into firing position, and the surveyors dismounted and prepared to advance in skirmishing order. The Gatling was stationed to the north, and Middleton rode out to within 400 yards of the Métis rifle pits to order the surveyors' advance. The rest of the infantry was kept hidden behind the advancing soldiers.

> The rebels evidently expected us, for we had only advanced a few yards when they must have caught sight of some of us over the rise, and a volley was fired into our ranks, at the report of which we dropped on our faces in the brush, one of us never again to rise again, for poor Kippen fell dead with a rifle bullet in his brain.[3]

The nine-pounder and the Gatling opened fire and there was a brief, intense exchange. The Métis were evidently expecting a major advance here. Middleton's tactics had worked.

Just as the Gatling was ready to be moved to a position farther north, Middleton saw a man riding toward him with a white flag. Astley, a surveyor captured by Riel just after the Battle at Duck Lake, "had just come from Riel, who was apparently in a great state of agitation, and handed me a letter from him in which he said, apparently referring to our shelling the houses, that if I massacred his women and children they would massacre their prisoners."[4] Middleton replied that he had no intention of deliberately injuring women and children, suggesting that they be placed in a building with a white flag flying from it, and Astley returned to the Métis headquarters with Middleton's answer.

It was now 11:30 a.m. and Middleton was ready to move back to camp. His deployment of troops seemed to have confused the Métis: "keeping us for a while just out of sight of the enemy, occasionally showing a mounted man or two to puzzle the rebels as to our movements, which always drew a volley from them."[5] The soldiers returned to camp having lost only one man in what had been intended to be an all-out advance by both Middleton's and Van Straubenzie's men against the Métis and Indians.

That morning Van Straubenzie had ordered the Midlanders and grenadiers out ready for an attack on the left flank when they heard the gunfire to the north; however, due to a strong east wind he heard none of the artillery or rifle fire from Middleton's contingent. When the general returned, Van Straubenzie pulled his men back slightly. Middleton was furious when he found that no attack had been made. "I am afraid on that occasion I lost both my temper and my head,"[6] although in retrospect Middleton thought that it was fortunate the charge had been aborted "for I believe the total silence and absence of fire from my left only strengthened the belief of the enemy that I was going to attack from the prairie ground."[7] The grenadiers and Midlanders were just completing their meal, "munching the bullet-proof discs of that indescribable compound known as Government biscuit,"[8] and Middleton was sitting down to his own meal when he gave a rather vague order to Van Straubenzie to "take them as far as he pleased."[9] The order may simply have been intended to send the men back to the positions they held that morning even though it might have been interpreted as a signal for a general advance against the Métis positions.

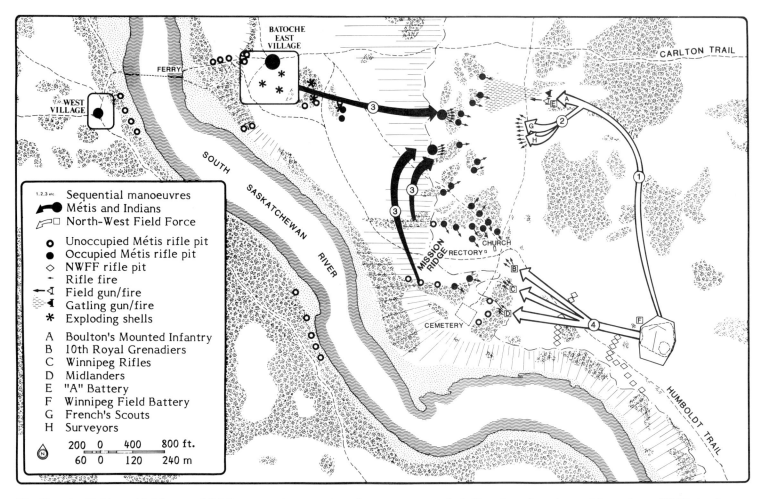

57 Day 4, 12 May, 10:00 a.m. Middleton again moved to the Jolie Prairie. Troops under Colonel Van Straubenzie were to attack the weakened southern flank of the Métis, but due to a strong wind, Van Straubenzie could not hear Middleton's guns and did not advance. (Map by B. Richard and D. Kappler.)

BATOCHE
EAST
VILLAGE
FERRY
WEST
VILLAGE
SOUTH
SASKATCHEWAN
RIVER
TRAIL TO ST. LAURENT
CARLTON TRAIL
JOLIE
PRAIRIE
FULL
RETREAT
CEMETERY
HUMBOLDT TRAIL
1,2,3 etc. Sequential manoeuvres
Métis and Indians
North-West Field Force
Unoccupied Métis rifle pit
Occupied Métis rifle pit
NWFF rifle pit
Rifle fire
Field gun/fire
Gatling gun/fire
Exploding shells
A Boulton's Mounted Infantry
B 10th Royal Grenadiers
C Winnipeg Rifles
D Midlanders
E "A" Battery
F Winnipeg Field Battery
G French's Scouts
H Surveyors
200 0 400 800 ft.
60 0 120 240 m

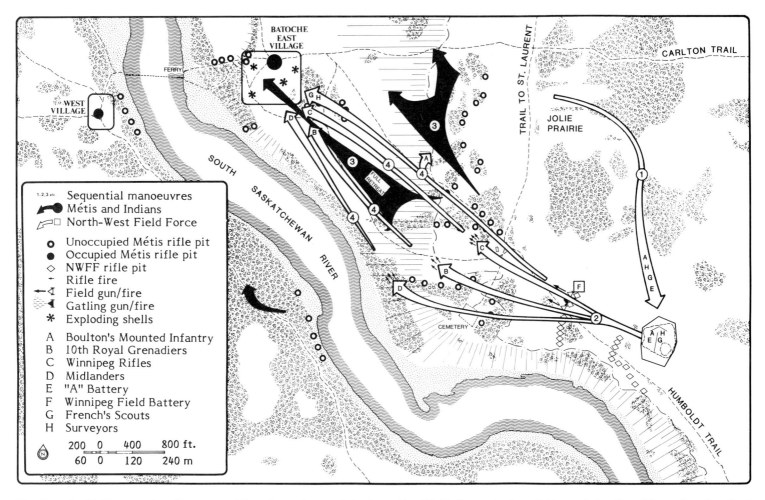

58 Day 4, 12 May, early afternoon. The planned attack had failed, but when the Métis had moved north from the pits around the church, they weakened the area enough to allow the Field Force to break through to the village for the final action. (Map by B. Richard and D. Kappler.)

The Métis were now desperately short of ammunition and fighting men. Of the original 250 to 300 combatants, only 50 to 60 men were fighting during the final battle, and only about 40 had rifles, "the rest had double-barrelled shotguns."[10] Some were firing nails when the bullets made from the spent bullets scavenged from the battlefield had been exhausted.

In addition, the Métis were confused by developments on the battlefield. When Middleton withdrew his men from the Jolie Prairie in the morning, many thought that peace had been declared, that Riel's message had won a cease-fire. "The cannon stops and Champagne runs out and shouts 'it's peace....' The Métis get up, sit on the edges of the pits ... then they get up and go back to the camp to their families, thinking peace had come."[11] It was, however, a terrible misunderstanding.

> We were washing up when Gabriel comes to send us back to the pits along the old road [the trail to St. Laurent] — we got there, and loud noise in the camp and gunshots — 10 minutes later, general battle. When the battle started again, there were 18 holding on, and many were running away one by one when they had a chance.[12]

Clearly, the disarray in which the Métis found themselves on that day was greater than has previously been believed.[13] The final attack by the Field Force was decisive even from the Métis perspective:

> we see the army coming from all sides in battle formation. Infantry, artillery, cavalry, all at once. With an order and purpose, a rapid movement that we had not seen the other days. At first look, we understood the hour of decision had come; that it was all over for Batoche.[14]

Riel was asked to perform the miracle he had promised his people, but to no avail.

> "Do your miracle now, it is time." Riel kneels, crosses his arms and starts to pray. Then he says: "People, 3 times we will say together very loudly: 'God have pity on us' "; Everyone kneels and prays. Then Riel continues. "Dear God, make those people stop, crush them," but the miracle did not happen. Riel asks two

men to hold his arms. Patrice, down on one knee, holding his gun, tells him to put his hand on his shoulder. Riel keeps praying (the soldiers' bullets are coming thick and dangerous). Riel goes down into the hollow of the coulee; Elie Dumont heard him lamenting to God and saw Patrice Tourond hold his hand.[15]

Conflicting accounts over exactly what happened after Middleton told Van Straubenzie to go "as far as he pleased" and who was responsible for the ensuing charge are numerous. Much of the controversy was motivated by those who sought personal glory and by those who either hated or admired Middleton. One account credits Colonel Williams with leading the final charge:

> one of the Midland men on the slope of the hill near the cemetery was hit by a volley from the west side of the river, and the ambulance men going to his relief were also fired upon. This seemed to infuriate the men, and their officers saw that there was no holding them any longer. Colonel Williams therefore decided upon charging and with only two companies of the Midland, he led the way counting on the 90th [Winnipeg Rifles] and the Grenadiers for support.[16]

Lieutenant Colonel Denison, who was not at the front but stationed at Humboldt, also acknowledged Williams as the leader of the final charge. Captain Peters of "A" Battery gave credit for the charge to Van Straubenzie, while Boulton tended to credit Middleton and Van Straubenzie with issuing the string of orders that led to the final charge.[17] Middleton's own description indicates that the breakthrough merely happened and was not actually ordered as an advance.

> After the men had had their dinners they were moved down to take up old positions and press on. Two companies of the Midland, 60 men in all ... were extended on the left and moved up to the cemetery, and the Grenadiers, 200 strong ... prolonged the line to the right beyond the church, the 90th [Winnipeg Rifles] being in support. The Midland and Grenadiers, led by Lt. Cols. Williams and Grassett, the whole led by Lt. Col. Straubenzie in command of the Brigade, then dashed forward with a cheer and drove the enemy out of the pits in front of the cemetery and the ravine to

59 *The Capture of Batoche.* The highly romanticized scene reflects the artist's desire to present the battle as an epic struggle. (Public Archives Canada, C-55581.)

60 Captain John French, formerly an inspector with the North-West Mounted Police, with men of the corps he raised in the Qu'Appelle area of southern present-day Saskatchewan to act as guides and scouts for Middleton. (Public Archives Canada, C-18942.)

6! Batoche's house. (Saskatchewan Archives Board, R-A 5634[1].)

the right of it, thus clearing the angle at the turn of the river.[18]

One theory suggests that because of the bend in the river it was necessary for the line of advance to curve to be equidistant from the rifle pits all along the front and that consequently the extreme left had to be ordered slightly forward. When so commanded they advanced without resistance, possibly due to weakly manned or vacant rifle pits for the Métis were now located to the north where attack was anticipated. Gaining confidence and momentum as they encountered little resistance, the extreme left broke into a run, and on seeing that movement, the rest of the front followed suit.

With a rush and a cheer they were down on the rebels with the fierceness of Bashi-Basouks, the Midland on the left, the Grenadiers in the centre, and the 90th on the right. The advance came sweeping round until but a few minutes saw the line of direction at right angles to the original line of attack. The cheering was that of satisfied and contented men, and the enthusiasm was intense. Nothing could have withstood the pace, the force, and the dogged determination of the men.[19]

Just as Middleton heard the cheers as the men broke through the first line of rifle pits, Astley, Riel's messenger, again appeared with a note from Riel: "General, — Your prompt answer to my note shows that I was right mentioning to you the cause of humanity. We will gather our families in one place and as soon as it is done we will let you know."[20] On the envelope was another missive, reflecting a more agitated state of mind: "I do not like the war, and if you do not retreat and [you] refuse an interview, the question remains the same concerning the prisoners."[21] Middleton ignored the messages; "of course no answer was sent."[22]

The advancing Midlanders, grenadiers and Winnipeg Rifles were now joined by men ordered by Middleton to extend the line to the right. One gun of "A" Battery and French's Scouts were also sent out. Boulton's Mounted lengthened the line even further, and the surveyors moved out to the right of Boulton's men. The artillery was now firing both at the village and at the Métis rifle pits across the river. In return, Métis fire was pouring down on the Midlanders closest to the river. At the same time both guns from the Winnipeg Field Battery and the Gatling opened fire on the village from the centre right of the front.

Stiff resistance was met as the column, "with the officers well in front,"[23] sped down the slopes toward the village. "The enemy poured in a hot fire when we started, but I don't think any of our men were hit until we got into the bush. Here many of the men were struck."[24]

We were pushing our way through the bush, which was pretty close, and jumping over the rifle pits, when [Fitch] was struck in the breast and in the corner of the eye. He fell with a groan and died immediately without speaking a word.... My heart jumped into my mouth when I saw him fall. I was then struck in the right arm but did not fall. I was disabled and dropped down, because the bullets were flying thick, and remained there until the men had gone ahead.... There were others hit in the bush about the same time.... The big guns did not begin firing until we got into the bush. When our men came to the rifle pits they found rebels who had not had time to get away in some of them.[25]

Captain French was killed when the troops drove the Métis and Indians out of the village. The 10th Royal Grenadiers, the Midlanders and French's Scouts were the first to arrive at the village. After capturing the stores they set their sights on Batoche's house, standing alone 100 yards from the village. The house was stormed and French dashed to the upper storey, hoping to fire at the retreating Métis. He appeared at a window and was struck by a bullet fired by "an old French half-breed, named Ross," who was immediately gunned down as he turned to escape.[26]

The battle was over "except for some desultory long-range firing, which was soon put down by two or three parties sent in different directions."[27] Middleton ordered the camp moved up. "I sent for our blankets and food, and bivouacked in and about the houses of the village, having, however, sent the scouts back to strengthen the guard I had left all day in the zareba under Lieutenant-Colonel Boswell, and a gun of A Battery."[28]

The prisoners were released. About 25 men had been confined since 10 March in a cellar, a piece of timber jammed between the ceiling and the trap door preventing any chance of escape.[29] They were various local residents and government employees taken as hostages and some of his own people Riel felt were disloyal, perhaps still held with the hope that he might be able to use them in negotiating a settlement.

The prisoners released from Batoche's house all bear the deep imprint of the hardships undergone during their long imprisonment, their pale, pinched faces and emaciated forms, furnishing indisputable proof of sufferings, both bodily and mental. They are easily picked out from among the many civilians about the camp, and it is moving to see their eagerness with which they grasp the hands of some acquaintance one or another they chance to meet. One of them is so overjoyed at being released that he shakes hands with everybody he approaches. Short rations, the close confinement, and the terrible suspense under which they lay, not knowing what moment might be their last, have done their work; and it will take weeks of care before their systems again recover their wonted vigour. One and all agree that but a short time longer and reason must have given way beneath the terrible strain.[30]

Prisoners taken during the fighting and the Métis women and children were found in an equally pitiful state. Terror of the artillery bombardment had driven them to the riverbanks. There "caves had been dug — ten, fifteen, twenty feet long, five or six wide, and four or five deep — and these were carefully covered with trees and brush and earth. In these, during the four days' struggle the families lived, and ate, and slept if they could."[31]

Property damage was extensive both from use by the Métis and from the artillery fire. Métis occupancy of Batoche's house left it in a shambles, while the Walters and Baker store was "an utter wreck, testifying to the destructiveness of heavy guns which played on it during the fight."[32] On his return to the village Georges Fisher found bullet holes inside and outside his store and the windows and sashes completely smashed.[33] As well, looting occurred on the 12th and the next day too:

> as the General's orders previously issued against [looting] could not be enforced, no interference was made. Some of the men needed articles of underwear, blacking, combs, etc., and these were hurriedly snatched. Guards were of course put on the stores, but the ill-assorted stores somehow or other disappeared. Trunks were ransacked and trophies of the war secured. The rebel state papers were found in the rebel council room....[34]

Even the personal belongings of some of the Métis women were taken: "Maurice Henry's wife, Donald Ross's daughter, was robbed right before his eyes, [they] opened her jewel case, took everything, even her wedding band. And when she cried out to have the ring back, they laughed at her and at her tears." And "they took everything from Baptiste Parenteau's wife ... left her only a shirt."[35]

At dusk on 12 May Middleton ordered the camp formed into a zareba. Located just to the north and east of Batoche's house, it was not as substantial as the zareba built on the 9th.[36] The precaution turned out to be unnecessary as no other shots were fired at Batoche.

AFTER THE BATTLE

The remainder of the campaign wound down rapidly. On 24 May Middleton reached Battleford, where Lieutenant Colonel Otter was stationed, and two days later Poundmaker gave himself up. On 27 May Major General Strange and Big Bear's Cree fought a brief, inconclusive battle at Frenchman's Butte. Middleton then set out to the Loon Lake area on 3 June in search of Big Bear, but gave up slogging through the bush by the 9th. Big Bear voluntarily surrendered at Fort Pitt on 2 July. This marked the end of Indian participation in the events of 1885. Even though many Easterners had believed otherwise, the actions of Poundmaker's and Big Bear's bands were never coordinated with those of the Métis.[1]

The Métis' will to resist further was gone as were their leaders. Riel surrendered to Middleton and the gallows; he was tried and hanged in Regina on 16 November. Gabriel Dumont and Michel Dumas escaped across the American border. Dumont spent some time as a sharpshooter in Buffalo Bill Cody's Wild West Show before returning to Batoche in 1890 where he died in 1906. The resistance by force was over and the men who had followed Riel and Dumont were now left to face trial and prison. The wave of settlement that Macdonald's National Policy had promised swept over the prairie.

In the days after the fighting at Batoche the men with the Field Force and the reporters with them talked to the Métis in the village. Over and over the soldiers and reporters heard accounts of how the Métis and their families had been forced to take up arms.

> All of them were sick of the "troubles;" all of them denounced Riel and Dumont; all of them wanted peace and home. It was curious, though, how unanimous they were in declaring that they had been pressed into service. Of over twenty with whom I conversed, not one had joined Riel willingly. To one he had threatened arrest; to another death; to a third the massacre

of his wife and children, if he failed to join the insurgents.... If what they said was true, and I am inclined to believe a good many of them, it only shows that Riel's organized few terrorized the unorganized many. But doubtless some of them lie.[2]

Boulton thought Riel's actions were those of a selfish man who tried to save his own life while exposing others to death.[3] An outraged Métis women wrote that Riel "is a woman. He stayed all day yesterday with the women and children, and he told the others to go and fight. He calls us women because we can't fight; but he is a woman himself."[4] Stories were told of Riel's religious claims and prophesies; for instance, Riel had told his people that he was the second messiah and that an army of Americans would save them.[5] Yet, even though their disillusion with Riel was great[6] and even though they recognized his errors in leading the fight, most of the Métis remained loyal to him.

Almost ten years later, reflecting upon the events of 1885, Middleton was generous in his praise of the fighting ability of the Métis and Indians. In his own mind, however, his choice of tactics was correct:

> needless to say, I was well satisfied with the result of the day's fighting, which proved the correctness of my opinion that these great hunters, like the Boers of South Africa, are only formidable when you play their game, "bush fighting," to which they are accustomed, but they cannot stand a determined charge.[7]

But a bold frontal attack had been possible not through anything Middleton or the Field Force did, but through Riel's determination to decide the Métis fate at Batoche. Fortunately for the Field Force, the guerilla tactics so effective at Fish Creek were not employed again.

The judgement of history has not been kind to Middleton. He had offended too many and too often. Men like Denison would record what they thought were Middleton's foibles and indiscretions, and newspapers published derisive commen-

62 Métis prisoners at the Regina court house (left to right): Jean Sansregret, Pierre Parenteau, Pierre Gariépy, Albert Monkman, Philippe Garnot, Pierre and Baptiste Vandale, Toussaint Lucier, Maxime Dubois, Timmus Short, Jean-Baptiste Tourond and Emmanuel Champagne. (Saskatchewan Archives Board, R-B 714.)

taries, no doubt inspired by disgruntled soldiers. Comparison can be made with Wolseley's Red River expedition in 1870: "Middleton presents an unfortunate contrast with Garnet Wolseley who, fifteen years before, led a mixed force of British regulars and Canadian militia to restrain the aberra-tions of the same Louis Riel, and in so doing won the intense and lasting loyalty of both."[8]

Most Westerners — those who rose in arms or those who were tempted to take arms or those who were passive — found a subtle irony in watching the changing attitudes of the

63 Wounded at Moose Jaw, June 1885. The Moose Hotel was requisitioned for use as a base hospital; twenty-eight wounded were treated there. Four nursing sisters of the Order of Saint John, Toronto, stand on the left, and three nurses from Toronto hospitals are on the right. (The Army Museum, Halifax Citadel.)

Eastern soldiers who came to suppress the rupture of discontent. Many who came with preconceived notions of the savage West changed their views; some compassionately grew to sympathize with the problems faced by those they had fought. The problems of administration in the North-West lay apparent to those who marched into the territory. Only after receiving reports from Eastern eyes in the distant North-West did many of the officials in Ottawa become aware of the extent of Western discontent and discover substance in Western complaints. This was evident in the

64 Wounded and sick officers and men after the battle.
(Public Archives Canada, C-18935.)

correspondence between Lord Melgund and Governor General Lansdowne even before the fighting broke out. For example, in response to a report from Melgund, Lansdowne wrote:

> you will be quite right in your idea that some thing must be done to keep the people from starvation that will be the next thing to look to. What an intricate problem it is. I am very anxious to talk to you about it.... I suspect that there is endless robbery and wrong doing on the spot. Do you think we could unearth any of their wrong doings? It would be a great thing if an example could be made of contractors who supply rotten beef.[9]

And to Lord Derby of the Foreign Office, Lansdowne wrote:

> the halfbreed grievance has been "simmering" for a long time in fact the halfbreeds have never been contented since the annexation of the N.W.T. to Canada. There has I should say been a disposition to deal with them liberally but these land claims are most difficult to adjust, and in some cases there has I have no doubt been well founded discontent occasioned by Ottawa red tape and procrastination.[10]

Melgund, later Earl of Minto and governor general of Canada, on whose observations both Lansdowne and Derby relied, understood the general discontent in the North-West among all groups as a result of neglect and inadequate administration.

> Riel and Gabriel Dumont were not counting only on their half-breed and Redskin rifles, but on the support of white men who [they] had been lulled into believing would stand by them. Riel put his fighting men in his first line, but in his second line we may perhaps find the disappointed white contractor, the disappointed white land shark, the disappointed white farmer.[11]

The tragedy that ended at Batoche was that the people Melgund mentioned, and especially the Métis and Indians who fought in the last battle, relied too heavily on Riel's military judgement to win redress for their grievances.

PART II
LEADERSHIP AND MILITARY TRADITIONS

The art of war is usually divided into two parts — strategy and tactics.... Broadly speaking ... strategy is concerned with the movement of troops before they come into actual collision, while tactics deal with the leading of troops in battle, or when battle is imminent. Strategy, moreover, seeks to derive from victory greater advantage than is to be obtained simply from defeating the enemy; it tries to place the victor in a position before the battle to gain the greatest effect possible from his tactical success when won.

Lieutenant Colonel Walter H. James, 1903.

RIEL AND DUMONT: THE STRATEGY TO DEFEND BATOCHE

It is misleading to speak of a military tradition among the Métis of Western Canada. They were not as warlike as the Plains Cree or the Dakota or even the whites who came to quash the resistance. Their fighting organization and tactics were characteristic of the buffalo hunt, which had always demanded a high degree of organization and discipline, qualities essential for survival in the harsh, demanding climate and terrain of Western Canada where failure in the hunt might lead to starvation and death. The Métis rarely in their history initiated warlike actions, but responded to those of others. Yet, though primarily defensive when threatened, the Métis did possess skills that were useful for attack. Some observers in the North-West "expressed surprise at the excellent discipline they maintained among themselves when on the grand annual buffalo hunt, and British Officers mentioned them in their reports as magnificent horsemen, and splendid marksmen, whose services would be invaluable in war on the frontier."[1]

The Métis inherited a number of fighting traditions from their Indian and European ancestors and learned others from their American neighbours. Their Indian heritage and their long experience on the land gave them a knowledge of using bush and coulees for both ambush and retreat, and they had inherited other fighting traditions from their English, Scottish or French forebears.[2] The lessons of the American Civil War might well have influenced the Métis at Batoche. But for the Métis, leadership more than anything else affected the outcome of the battle and, ultimately, of the whole resistance.

There is general agreement among historians who have written about the events of 1885 that Riel was not initially committed to a military solution, but hoped to compel the federal government to resolve the grievances of Western Canadians.[3] Riel, as he had been earlier, was the political spokesman for the Métis people in 1885, and he sought to accomplish his goal in a fashion similar to the way he had won victory for the Métis in Red River in 1869-70: by taking hostages and bargaining from a position of power. He hoped that the conflict between the federal government and the Métis would conclude in a negotiated settlement. But his initial goal to have Métis grievances solved by using hostages as a bargaining lever was rendered useless by Macdonald, who was now determined not to negotiate with those in the West who were defying his government's authority. Macdonald's resolve not to bargain with the Métis forced them into a military resolution of the conflict, a path they may not have initially wanted.

This is not to suggest that Riel was the cause of the outbreak of violence. Whether Riel was politically skilled enough to have prevented alone the outbreak of violence in the North-West is one of those nagging but unanswerable "what ifs" of history, but — while this account is not directly concerned with detailing the political causes of the Métis resistance — it is probably safe to say that the social and economic disruption the Métis faced as the fur-trade economy declined and was replaced by Macdonald's National Policy and the industrial society that pushed it westward was the greatest single cause of the conflict. The social and economic displacement, though perhaps less obvious during the immediacy of the fighting, was far more significant than any one man's personality, even personalities as large and dominant as Macdonald's or Riel's. Nevertheless, *militarily* Riel's personality was a factor in the outcome of the Battle of Batoche.

In the 15 years since the uprising in Red River, circumstances in the North-West had changed. So had Macdonald and so had Riel. Prime Minister Macdonald was more intransigent, and the Canadian Pacific Railway now traversing the West assured easier troop movement than in 1869-70. Moreover, the power of the federal government had to be asserted. If settlement of the Canadian prairies was to proceed as planned, Western defiance had to be put down as

65 Louis Riel shortly after his capture. (Public Archives
Canada, C-3450.)

an example to others. Riel's bluff had been called. He had not allowed a slaughter at Duck Lake or harassment of Middleton's column after Fish Creek. He continuously cautioned his followers not to inflict unnecessary death on the encroaching militia. His tendency to cautious action had repercussions for the Métis in the strategy he chose for Batoche. The only guerilla action that Riel had allowed against the Field Force — at Fish Creek — was not enough to defeat them.

By contrast Dumont proposed that more forceful action be taken against crucial centres in the North-West, where the authority of Eastern Canada was most evident. Dumont had suggested early attacks on Fort Carlton, Prince Albert and Battleford to take the supplies and ammunition needed to cripple the awkward columns of the North-West Field Force. Scouts would be sent out on either side of the South Saskatchewan River to determine the position of the columns and the Métis would then ambush the soldiers on ground and at times that the Métis would choose, when the columns were most vulnerable. In the tradition of the buffalo hunt, captains would command small but disciplined groups of hunters, now soldiers.

Dumont was confident that such bold actions would gain the Métis the support of the Indians and English-speaking mixed bloods. He was uneasy about Riel's intention to defend the cause at Batoche. When Dumont was overruled, he did what he could to resist the Canadian militia. In later years Dumont said that he acquiesced to Riel's plans reluctantly, but felt compelled by Riel's religious power:

> we were then 350 men all told, of whom 200 were armed. I proposed we go ahead of troops, harass them by night, and above all prevent them from sleeping, believing that this was a good way to demoralize them and make them lose heart. But Riel did not agree, saying that this was too much like the Indians, and that besides we might be in danger of firing on our [French-]Canadian friends. For my part I would have done so without scruple, and I would even willingly have blown up the railway, because it wouldn't consider as his friends those who joined the English, to kill and plunder us. Riel used to tell me: "If you knew

66 Gabriel Dumont joined Buffalo Bill's Wild West Show after the fighting at Batoche. Photo *circa* 1887. (Public Archives Canada, PA-117943.)

them, you wouldn't try to treat them in that way." Be that as it may, we were obliged to give up the idea of meeting our enemies on ground favourable to us, and, I am sure, we should have made them so edgy that at the end of three nights they would have been at each other's throats. I yielded to Riel's judgement although

I was convinced that from a humane standpoint, mine was the better plan; but I had confidence in his faith and his prayers and that God would listen to him.[4]

The Métis as a people had seldom been attacked throughout their history, certainly never by a regular army. Dumont's and Riel's contrasting opinions on how to best deal with an army showed their inexperience in such matters. While Riel reflected the traditional Métis response to entrench when threatened, Dumont intuitively sensed that a more offensive strategy was needed for the circumstances the Métis now faced. A combination of mobility and discipline had been successful for the Métis in the buffalo hunt, although they had very rarely used such tactics in a military confrontation until Duck Lake and Fish Creek, their greatest military successes. But mobility was lost when they retreated into a defensive shell at Batoche. Métis strategy and tactics were inextricably linked to leadership, and it was Riel's defensive plan that prevailed.

After 1869-70, Riel increasingly withdrew to a bizarre world of his own,[5] battered by his experiences, severely affected by the aftermath of the Red River resistance and still haunted by his father's death in 1864. In 1876-77 for a little more than a year and a half Riel spent time in the Beauport asylum just outside Quebec City. He believed he could manipulate the world at his command. He was increasingly attracted to the speculative world of theology, but the local Roman Catholic clergy rejected his schemes, apprehensive about his political goals. Father Fourmond described Riel's complex behaviour:

> we decided not to meet with him anymore. One would think that he has a tic about politics. Reasons well and politely about everything else, a religious man, full of devotion and altruism, seemingly obedient to the clergy, he is completely the opposite about political issues, at least on the North West question. He has all the manners and ideas of a real revolutionary and demagogue, respecting neither common sense nor authority, seeing himself as a real statesman and wishing as such to impose his plans and ideas upon all without considering any prudent counsel, believing all

the strangest and most deadly illusions, ready to overcome all obstacles ahead of him, invoking the voice of his mistaken conscience to justify the most extreme measures. To excuse him, some feel sorry for him and blame these deviations on the irritability of nerves caused by the long opposition, persecution, injustices, and all sorts of misfortunes he has suffered. Others blame his slips of behaviour on his demented imagination, which are quickly put aside because of his kind heart. More than once, after behaving in a regrettable way toward the clergy, we saw him kneeling before the superior humbly asking for his forgiveness and religious benediction. Still others think that he lets himself go to these excesses in the interest of his cause, having no other aim but to scare his adversaries and opponents with these threats and to make them repent.[6]

The clergy's attitude to Riel had an impact on the entire resistance. Alex Fisher, the ferryman at Batoche, educated at St. Boniface College and connected to the fur trade through his uncle Henry Fisher, a chief trader of the Hudson's Bay Company, reiterated what others said, that if the clergy had backed the Métis as they had in 1869-70 at Red River, it would have boosted Métis morale, drawing more Métis to action.[7]

Psychohistorians have argued that Riel projected his own psychological problems onto the events around him and wanted to rearrange the entire world after visions he had seen: "By [1885] he was referring to himself as 'The Prophet of the New World,' whose every thought and action was determined by the spirit of God through the Holy Ghost."[8] Riel was not totally incapacitated; he understood what was happening around him. But he was indecisive and showed an ambiguity toward his "enemies" during the campaign. There is indeed evidence that he did not want to see others die: he had not allowed his men to pursue the retreating police at Duck Lake, and he was reluctant to attack the approaching columns of the Field Force since he believed that among them would be French-Canadians. He seemed especially concerned with impending retribution. It is not surprising that he was apprehensive; Riel was again challenging established authority including the federal government and the church.

Riel was not just the Métis political leader, he was also a spiritual leader who possessed a special personal appeal.[9] Alex Fisher admired Riel's leadership abilities even though he was not unquestioning: "as far as politics go I think Riel was a really competent man but in regard to religion he pushed it to fanaticism and I think that is what was disturbing his head and prevented him from paying attention to the real cause that he had the Métis fighting for."[10] To assess Métis military strategy coldly without appreciating Riel's influence would leave a great gap in the story. Riel was charismatic. The energy that came from the tension in his personality impressed many around him and convinced them that his visions were ordained by God.[11] He moved people by emotion and as a leader attracted them by a personal charm. Fisher, who recognized that the Métis were sometimes manipulated by Riel, could still not think of a better leader for them: "because I believe and am almost certain that this man had the Métis cause at heart and that he was the only man who had worked for the welfare of the nation."[12]

But Riel's temperament in 1885 was ill-suited for the kind of leadership the Métis needed, and his instability increased as the stress of fighting escalated. Throughout the months of the fighting Riel prayed for salvation and assured his people that they would be delivered from death:

> the Spirit of God who is infinitely good and to whom I continually give thanks told me something consoling. I cannot remember the exact words He used, but I can announce the good news for Him; for help is coming to us. The Spirit of the Good Lord even condescended to let me know that He was rushing to help us.[13]

Riel, more dominant than the realist Dumont, believed that at Batoche the Métis would be saved from certain death by the hand of God. It was Riel's influence that was ultimately responsible for the nature and severity of the defeat they suffered.

The strategy Riel chose for his people at Batoche was inappropriate for the circumstances they faced. It is easy to speculate on the Métis strategy with hindsight, yet almost without exception, those who have written about the resistance suggest that a more offensive strategy familiar from the days of the buffalo hunt might have changed the course of history for the Métis and the North-West:

> For if Riel had agreed to Dumont's plans, there is a fair probability that the ill-defended positions of Fort Carlton and Prince Albert would have been taken without difficulty, with Battleford to follow shortly afterwards, and that the English half-breeds would have joined the winning side.[14]

Yet even had the Métis listened to Dumont, they would have had little chance of a military victory over the soldiers of the North-West Field Force: there were simply too many soldiers and, behind the soldiers, the power and determination of the federal government. But perhaps Riel's hope for a negotiated truce could have been attained if he had been backed by a record of guerrila successes across the North-West, if he had not chosen Batoche as the place where the Métis would make their stand.

When threatened, the Métis could quickly move to defend themselves.

> The hunt would go into a lager [sic]. The carts would be formed into a circle, surrounding the stock and women. The barricade would be strengthened with poles and ropes, to prevent stock stampeding, for without them the party was lost. Then some picked men would ride out to skirmish, the others would lie out from the cart-circle behind rocks or in gun-pits to hold the enemy out of range, so that they could not shoot horses in the lager. The Métis marksmen could usually pick off enough Indians to discourage any bold advance on the camp. And after the foe had withdrawn, the march would continue in four columns, ready instantly to wheel into a square to stand off a return of the Sioux.[1]

While this response was successful against the Indians, it would not be successful against Middleton's determined militia. Some military actions had been known in the North-West, such as the confrontation between the Métis and territorial governor Semple and his men at Seven Oaks (within present-day Winnipeg) in 1816, but even there the action was spontaneous and short-lived rather than carefully planned. Lengthy battles rarely occurred on the prairies.

The influence of traditional Plains Indian tactics was evident in the battle tactics the Métis chose. It could be seen in their ambush methods and use of the terrain at Duck Lake, Fish Creek and Batoche. Indians had traditionally practised horse-raiding techniques that were sound training for guerilla warfare but not for a lengthy confrontation:

> Prolonged wars, standing armies, and officers holding permanent rank were lacking. The objective was never to acquire new land. Though it did happen that major tribal forces were pitted against each other, this rarely happened in the usual ... adventure involving only a few warriors. It was considered of the utmost importance that a party return without the loss of a man; deliberately to incur losses for strategic ends was wholly repulsive to Indian ideas.[2]

The broader principles inherent in Indian war practices applied to the mixed bloods. However, the Métis had no tradition of horse stealing as a form of seeking status, they were not generally warlike, nor were they extensively involved in battle for the sake of preserving a tradition of glory. Only with the Dakota did they have any long-standing feuds on the plains and those had ended in 1851 with the Battle of Grand Coteau in North Dakota.

The Battle of Grand Coteau reflected Métis ability to respond rapidly when threatened. In their seasonal pursuit of the buffalo the Métis found it necessary to ride into Dakota territory. In the spring of 1851 the Dakota were waiting for them. As soon as the Dakota attacked, the Métis swiftly moved to form a laager.

> Carts were pulled in a circle, wheel to wheel, with the shafts tilted in the air. Poles carried to make frames on which buffalo-meat was dried were run through the spokes to make the carts immovable. Packs, hides, saddles and dried meat were piled between and under the carts to complete the barricade.[3]

At Grand Coteau the Métis held out for two days without losing a single life and with only three wounded, showing a remarkable ability to respond quickly and effectively.

Other tactics the Métis used at Grand Coteau included the digging of rifle pits, and that, too, can attributed to traditional Indian tactics. There is evidence that Indians used rifle pits as well as more elaborate, permanent defences. In the eighteenth century, explorer Alexander Henry described Saulteaux entrenchments:

> there were three principal ones, about 25 feet long, 5 feet wide, and 4 feet deep. These were intended for men to defend themselves in, whilst the women and children would lie close on the bottom. I was surprised

to see how expeditious they were, having neither hoes nor spades, they made use of their axes to cut the earth, and both women and children with their hands threw it into kettles, and others into blankets and toss it up. The Indian women and children lay in the trenches all night, the men in their cabins [sic].[4]

The Dakota were also known to have used rifle pits for defensive purposes. One site on the plains

> is an unbroken prairie sod and is quite well preserved. A circle of holes about 2' x 6' and 2-1/2' deep and big enough to hold 2 men in a crouching position were dug with the dirt thrown up on the outside. They enclose an area about 100 yds across. There were small gaps of 2 - 3' between the holes. Back of the circle about 12' every little way was a pair of round holes a little deeper.[5]

Entrenchment tactics adopted by the Confederate Army during the American Civil War (1861-65) might well have influenced the Métis. Perhaps Riel became aware of this aspect of the war while he was in exile in the United States from 1870 to 1885, when he had occasion to discuss the war with Edward Mallet, a major who had fought in the Civil War and whom Riel met on a friendly basis in Washington in 1874. The construction of the Métis rifle pits were certainly elaborate and stout enough to indicate that they were consciously part of the Métis plans for Batoche.[6] They were not simple, shallow dugouts; they were five to six feet deep, had solid, horizontal-timber breastworks, and could hold up to ten men. The pits gave the Métis a chance to succeed against a numerically superior enemy.

Tactics used during the American Civil War set patterns for subsequent land warfare. Both the Confederates and the Métis were significantly outnumbered, and in the long run both had to abandon dreams of victory and simply hope the opposition could be forced to stop its advance. But technology had given outnumbered men, if their positions were secure, an advantage over their enemies. Bayonet charges and other infantry tactics usually benefitting an army of greater numbers than its opponents were no longer as devastating as they had been in the heyday of the musket. Rifles, longer ranged and more accurate than muskets, could cripple frontal assaults. In theory the consequences favoured the Métis: "individual ... shooting ... for full effectiveness ... demanded individual initiative and collective loose order."[7] The evolution of the rifle meant that field entrenchment was necessary. It is with that tactic that the Métis, like the Confederates, had so much success.

The North-West Field Force was repeatedly checked at both Fish Creek and Batoche when infantry charges bogged down against strategically placed Métis and Indian sharpshooters, tactics that certainly impressed Middleton. The Métis defensive alignment was the dominant factor in the four-day battle at Batoche. As the military historian Fuller has written in the *The Conduct of War,*

> the spade increasingly became the complement of the rifle, until in 1864, every battle fought between Grant and Lee in the wilderness of Virginia was an entrenched one, and when Grant neared Petersburg and Richmond, both sides became so extensively entrenched that siege warfare set in and lasted for nearly ten months.... It was the rifle bullet and the spade which made the defensive the stronger form of war.[8]

Other military experts also noted this advantage: "put a man in a hole ... and a good battery on a hill behind him, and he will beat off three times his number, even if he is not a very good soldier."[9] For the Métis this worked for the first three days. Unfortunately for the Confederates and now the Métis, neither supplies nor manpower could be maintained, and the Métis had made no plans to withdraw and regroup under more favourable circumstances. By the fourth day of fighting the odds against them were more than 16 to one.

67 A Métis rifle pit after the battle. (Glenbow Archives, Calgary, NA-363-49.)

From planning the strategy to executing it, Macdonald, Caron and Middleton faced difficulties that cannot always be appreciated without understanding the economic constraints and the transport, leadership and supply problems. Some of these issues have been singled out for discussion below.

As Métis strategy was significantly affected by Riel's personality, so the North-West Field Force's approach was influenced by Middleton's training and experience. Born in Britain, Middleton exuded the confidence that was typical of graduates of Sandhurst, Britain's renowned military school. From 1874 to 1884 he was commandant at Sandhurst. He had a significant influence on that institution and was remembered as "an engaging and energetic man who would be incessantly seen striding about the College in peg-top overalls. He had a pretty dark-haired [French-]Canadian wife."[1] In July 1884 Middleton was named commander of the Canadian militia; he was Caron's personal choice for the post.[2] Convinced of British superiority in all things, Middleton was the total Victorian Englishman.

Although Middleton assumed a Canadian office in 1884, he openly scorned Canadian officers. In the North-West campaign he generally appointed British senior officers instead of Canadians. Middleton would eventually pay the price in

68 Sir Frederick Middleton in 1886 in the full-dress uniform of a major general of the British Army. He is wearing the insignia of the Order of Saint Michael and Saint George, with the Order of the Bath and the knighthood he was awarded for his services during the rebellion, as well as campaign medals for New Zealand, the Indian Mutiny and the newly issued North-West Canada medal. (Public Archives Canada, PA-26733.)

reputation for his stubbornness. Lieutenant Colonel Denison, overlooked for promotion by Middleton in 1885, later got satisfaction in writing:

> General Middleton had to leave Canada under a cloud, through the action of Parliament, which charged him with having appropriated a large number of furs belonging to a half-breed. The General was rather harshly treated in this matter, for he was only acting in accordance with a common practice in storming a place in the hands of an enemy. In this case, however, it was pretty clearly shown that the owner of these furs was not a rebel.[3]

Denison took further enjoyment in portraying Middleton shortly before his death:

> I saw him again in 1897 ... at luncheon at Lady Wolseley's. He seemed well and in good spirits, but very indignant at the way in which everyone was paying attention to the visitors from the outer Empire, particularly at the great deference shown to the Indian dignitaries who, when he was in India, he said, had to pay deference to him. I made the remark that it was the Colonial year, and that we were having our turn, that next year it would be somebody else.... General Middleton then told about his being at some entertainment where some third rate Indian dignitary was present, who wanted to get rid of his outer cloak. When a lady said to him, "Sir Frederick, won't you take his Highness' coat?" Certainly not, Madame" said General Middleton, and he seemed very indignant that anyone should have made such a suggestion to him.[4]

In the North-West Middleton's preconceptions had a significant impact on strategy planning: units led by Canadian officers were generally given assignments away from possible combat. For example, Denison, commander of the Governor General's Body Guard and author of a book on cavalry warfare, was stationed at Humboldt.[5] (Although Middleton has often been criticized for excluding Denison, he may deliberately have kept the cavalry away from the battles because of its tendency to charge its objective directly. The mounted infantry that Middleton chose to rely on would have been much easier to control and less likely to charge into a disastrous predicament.[6]) Other Canadian officers were likewise stationed outside the principal area of conflict. When Otter, later to become the first Canadian commander of the Canadian militia, took the initiative against Poundmaker's Cree at Cut Knife Hill he was severely reprimanded by Middleton. In the Battle of Batoche Middleton tended to delegate assignments that could result in military victories to British-led corps. Some observers later claimed that the general was reluctant to acknowledge that the final breakthrough at Batoche was led by the Canadian Lieutenant Colonel Arthur Williams and instead recognized the British Lieutenant Colonel Van Straubenzie.[7] While Middleton's preference for experienced British officers may be understandable, at the very least it created discontent among the Canadian troops.

Another result of Middleton's attitude toward Canadians was his blatant disregard for the North-West Mounted Police, which knew the territory and its inhabitants so well. Middleton kept the police, who were under his command, away from the action, and satirized what he believed were their exaggerated calls for assistance from Prince Albert and Battleford where they were protecting the white populations. Middleton thought the police were panicking.

> On [1 and 2 April] I received rather alarming news from Battleford, the mounted police officer in command there being evidently a pessimist, and from what I could gather, I do not believe Battleford was in any such danger as he described, but I telegraphed to Lieutenant-Colonel Herchmer at Regina to hurry to Battleford with his party of mounted police, and one mountain gun.[8]

In a critical commentary on Middleton's attitude toward the police the historian G.H. Needler wrote:

> Middleton showed throughout great lack of understanding of their character and of the desperate situation with which they were suddenly confronted. Their strength was hopelessly inadequate for doing what he blandly expected of them.[9]

Middleton's was an unwarranted assessment of the police whose presence in the North-West up to 1885 was respected by the native populations. It was not until Fish Creek that

Middleton understood that he had underestimated his enemy, and he too became more wary of the situation ahead.

Much of the popular literature that followed the campaign was written by Canadians and was critical of Middleton's tactics at Fish Creek and Batoche because of his favoritism. Although a more tolerant personality might have lessened the petty rivalries among officers, in the panorama of the campaign some of the observations made about Middleton were unfair in their emphasis. For example, Middleton's initial determination to advance against the enemy with the utmost haste proved a decisive factor in the campaign's success. His detractors ignored the energy he showed in mobilizing and dispatching his men in spite of political wrangling, transportation barriers, communication breakdowns, an unrelenting climate, difficult terrain and unseasoned troops.

The basic strategy of the North-West Field Force was simple and more defined than that of the Métis: to get to the theatre of war as quickly as possible. Communication, supply lines and the cost of the campaign played an integral part in the overall strategy adopted. Getting to the scene proved as important as the subsequent fighting. The foremost political consideration was the simple matter of cost, evident from the telegrams exchanged between Caron and Middleton. In 1884 the government had saved $74 121 through cutbacks to funding to the North-West, a factor contributing to the discontent.[10] (The total cost of the campaign was five million dollars and the death of over a hundred men.[11]) Ironically, saving money was still the primary concern of Adolphe Caron as minister of Militia and Defence, and it significantly influenced the campaign. Middleton, sensitive to Caron's parsimony, moved against the insurgents with as much haste as circumstances allowed.

More concrete problems confronted the officers and men. For virtually all of the three thousand men who came west over the uncompleted line, that week of travel was the most arduous phase of the campaign. For men who, only a few days before, had been office clerks, shopkeepers and factory hands, it was a fierce introduction to the hardships of campaigning. Packed in open railway cars, they endured temperatures that went far below zero. Their food when they got it, was salt pork, biscuit and unsweetened tea. For days on end, in freezing weather, they were hungry, sleepless and wet.... Arthur Potvin ... a young medical student from Laval, recalled that the bitter cold even drove him to thought of suicide. One unfortunate man in the 65th actually did try to throw himself under a railway car while a soldier in the 10th Royal Grenadiers went insane, threw off his clothes and tried to throw himself on a bonfire.[12]

The extreme conditions of the late winter made such stories common. The soldiers also had to face the incomplete railroad north of Lake Superior, covering the line on foot or by dog sled. Nevertheless, military observers have generally viewed the movement of men as successful. As one wrote to Caron, "you ought to feel proud of the manner in which your troops have performed the march by Lake Superior. It would do credit to the best organized regular force in the world and is worthy of note historically."[13]

Managing resources along with his troops was a major problem and one that commentators agree Middleton handled competently too. Coping with problems of supply and organization in such a vast territory presented serious difficulties for a government embarking on its first war without direct assistance from Britain.[14] As one military historian noted,

it is clear that Administration dominated the campaign. Once considerable forces were brought to bear on the centres of the rising, the result was not in doubt; but concentrating and maintaining those forces was a very heavy administrative task. The fact that the movement of the troops from the East over the unfinished Canadian Pacific, and the transport for the columns in the theatre of operations itself, were successfully improvised, is much to the credit of all concerned. However, had the Militia possessed a proper staff and supply organization, improvisation would have been unnecessary, money would have been saved, and there would have been less risk of calamity.[15]

69 "Cold Comfort in a Flat Car," *The Illustrated War News,* Vol. 1, No. 3, 18 April 1885. 10th Royal Grenadiers in open railway cars en route to the North-West. Though perhaps somewhat overdramatized, this and the following drawing do indicate the considerable hardships that the troops suffered. (Public Archives Canada, C-7683.)

70 " 'A' Battery in the Touchwood Hills — Stuck in a Snow-Bank," *The Illustrated War News,* Vol. 1, No. 3, 18 April 1885. (Public Archives Canada, C-11537.)

71 Red River carts drawn by horses and mules with civilian teamsters leaving Swift Current in 1885 to carry supplies to the Queen's Own Rifles. The photograph illustrates the main logistical problems of the campaign: primitive transport, poor roads and long distances. (The Army Museum, Halifax Citadel.)

72 Ox-drawn transport wagons escorted by infantry, probably men of the York and Simcoe Battalion, in the Touchwood Hills. (Saskatchewan Archives Board, R-A 441.)

73 Fording the South Saskatchewan River. (Saskatchewan Archives Board, R-B 2067; copy on file, Public Archives Canada.)

74 Moving troops and supplies by ferry. (Public Archives
Canada, C-4592.)

MIDDLETON'S TACTICS IN RETROSPECT

At the end of the campaign Middleton was considerably criticized for his tactics, criticisms that were to haunt him until he left Canada in 1896. His decisions were seen to have delayed the eventual outcome and contributed to the high costs of the expedition. The splitting of his troops at Clark's Crossing, his use of the zareba, and the apparent failure of his feinting movements at Batoche have all been cited as examples of his incompetence.[1] But none of his critics have tried to place his actions within the accepted fighting traditions of the British army in the nineteenth century. Colonel Garnet J. Wolseley's *The Soldier's Pocket-book for Field Service,* first published in 1869, provides the basis for justifying many of Middleton's decisions, even his nondeployment of Denison's cavalry.[2] Moreover, an authority on frontier warfare singled out Middleton's tactics as worthy of recognition. In *Small Wars,* published in 1896, Captain Charles Callwell compiled the wide variety of tactics acceptable when conducting wars against native populations.[3] The book is a rarity since the British seldom recorded their traditions but instead tended to pass them on through practice.

Callwell's treatise discusses almost all of the tactics Middleton chose to follow. His decisions were militarily sound in the context of small wars practice. Callwell elucidated on the nature and conduct of small wars:

> practically [small] wars may be said to include all campaigns other than those where both opposing sides consist of regular troops. It comprises the expeditions against savages and semi-civilized races by disciplined soldiers, campaigns undertaken to suppress rebellions and guerilla warfare in all parts of the world where organized armies were struggling against opponents who will not meet them on the open field. It thus obviously covers operations very varying in their scope and conditions.[4]

In the purview of "small wars," flexibility and creativity were prerequisites.[5] At Fish Creek the need to change tactics in the face of the accurate and heavy fire power of the Métis abated when the Métis withdrew and Middleton formed a zareba to protect his men and care for the 55 wounded. But at Batoche Middleton did improvise and show flexibility after initial, direct attacks failed. After facing a wall of resistance on both the 9th, when his infantry were able to move to the church and rectory, and again on the 10th, when they were not able to regain their previous position, Middleton began employing diversionary tactics that eventually proved successful.

Callwell stated that factors taken for granted in conventional warfare present an army with significant difficulties on a frontier.[6] Lack of information concerning geography and location of even the theatre of war can present serious obstacles for a regular army. The resulting battle against nature often leads to supply problems and poorly fed troops. Middleton and the North-West Field Force had to face all of these problems and Middleton coped remarkably well in the circumstances.

Once environmental obstacles had been surmounted, Callwell saw — as have great generals since warfare began — taking and maintaining initiative as essential. While recognizing the necessity of gaining an early advantage, Callwell advised that an army should not advance too soon. "The great point to aim at is not so much that there should be no delay in getting into motion as that once in motion there should be no check. An ephemeral triumph is dearly purchased at the cost of a subsequent period of discreditable inaction."[7] Middleton seems to have been well aware of this principle though it might be argued that he could have held off his advance until he had more troops with him. For example, Otter's force might have given him the advantage at Fish Creek. But Middleton was able to regroup his men and regain the initiative after Fish Creek. He knew the grave implications that a victory against his forces might have for Métis and Indian morale; he had seen evidence of a domino effect when, following the Battle of Duck Lake, a band of Cree attacked the Frog Lake settlement.

Sustaining the initiative was considered important since natives were believed to be easily affected by immediate, direct action. In chapter entitled "Boldness and Vigour: The Essence of Effectively Conducting such Operations," Callwell cited reasons for that approach:

> it is a cardinal principle ... that the initiative must be maintained, that the regular army must lead while its adversaries follow, that the enemy must be made to feel a moral inferiority throughout. The lower races are.... greatly influenced by a resolute bearing and a determined course of action.... The spectacle of an organized body of troops sweeping forward slowly but surely into their territory unnerves them. There must be no doubt as to who controls the general course of the war; delays must not occur, they cause the enemy to pluck up courage; every pause is interpreted as weakness, every halt gives new life to the foe.[8]

Furthermore, Callwell stated that it is better to fight immediately than to wait; time favours the enemy.[9] Even after the disastrous charge of the Light Brigade, British military experts confidently believed that bold frontal confrontations with the enemy were essential: such displays of pluck and courage should at once impress and demoralize the enemy forces. Similarly, the infantry tactics Middleton employed early in the fighting were attempts to secure a sudden victory.

Some have criticized Middleton for not proceeding with more direct tactics, but again Middleton's diversionary tactics after he was checked at Batoche were within the acceptable theory of fighting small wars as outlined by Callwell. Callwell began his discussion of feints by stating that they are often used by native forces, in which cases they are indicative of native characters: "Orientals have an inborn love of trickery and deception. The Red Indians have won an evil notoriety by their duplicity and craftiness."[10] (What feints by Europeans indicated about their characters was a point Callwell did not cover.) Callwell explained that the success of feinting by a European army results from the natives' over-confidence, which prevents them from appreciating the flexibility of "regular armies." In Callwell's sterotyped image, natives were apt to find the sight of an invading regular army ridiculous and to lose caution against what appeared to be a cumbersome, easy target.[11] Callwell held up Middleton's manoeuvres at Batoche as an example of a successful feint, "carried out in very effective fashion."[12]

Following the campaign, Middleton was considerably criticized for his use of zarebas at Fish Creek and Batoche. The intensity of the criticism was in part due to Middleton's general unpopularity and to his reluctance to discuss his tactics, especially with his Canadian officers. The Canadian criticism was also due in part to an overzealous desire for battle and for defeating the Métis in a face-to-face confrontation, especially after the two-week slow-down following Fish Creek; however, after Fish Creek, Middleton was skeptical about his men's ability to manoeuvre under fire and zarebas were sound tactics in the circumstances.[13]

Striking quickly and decisively was always Middleton's desired objective. Though many believed that the zareba was only a defensive tactic that interrupted momentum, the theory behind the use of this tactic was actually more sophisticated and was compatible with Middleton's objectives. Callwell wrote that zarebas can be used in numerous circumstances and that they "possess from the tactical point of view all the attributes of fortification, their employment means a defensive attitude — an attitude tending indeed toward passive defense."[14] A zareba could have a negative effect on men who believed it was being employed because they were unable to defeat the foe in open confrontation, and this point of morale was conceded by Callwell; however, he argued that it might be outweighed by the advantages of zarebas.

A zareba is a basically defensive tactic within an overall offensive campaign.[15] It originated with pioneers, who came to a frontier in wagons and used circle formations in the face of hostile natives. The Métis were certainly familiar with it. In regular military tactics it stems from the square. It was recommended when a long column of transport needed to be guarded and when fighting guerrillas. Callwell also advocated using it, especially among bushes, when an army was approaching an enemy of unknown strength. All of these circumstances confronted Middleton. Callwell particularly recommended it in South Africa and North America, and specifically cited Middleton's use of zarebas as an example of proper use of the tactic: "in the campaign against Riel ... the regular army has adopted it to varying circumstances with great success."[16]

At Batoche the zareba was essential: it allowed Middleton to regroup his men at night. It did not, as some have claimed, significantly delay the general pace of the campaign. In fact, had he not resorted to the zareba, he might have suffered the same fate as the British army at Isandhlwana where, by failing to regroup after covering substantial distance and by overextending their lines, the British suffered a devastating defeat at the hands of the Zulus in 1878. After Isandhlwana British armies were ever conscious of the importance of soundly protecting their night encampments. It was the best tactic Middleton could have adopted.

Middleton received perhaps the most severe criticism for splitting his troops at Clark's Crossing and moving north on both sides of the South Saskatchewan. It was condemned as a major military blunder, partly because it has been assumed that Middleton would have fared better at Fish Creek if he had been accompanied by Montizambert and his 370 men. But again there was basis for his action and again it can be found in Callwell, whose basic point was that strategy and tactics in regular warfare and "small wars" differ, sometimes dramatically.

Middleton's intention in splitting his troops was to make sure that he engaged as many of the rebels as possible as quickly as possible. Although this is not recommended in a regular campaign, in small wars "separation in the field is often a necessary consequence of the conditions of the campaign, for in struggles of this nature there frequently is more than one objective."[17] It was particularly justifiable in guerilla warfare where it may overwhelm the enemy: "there can be no doubt that the spectacle of several well appointed columns of regular troops pouring into their territory alarms semi-civilized races and savages more than would a simple army, and for this reason division of force is often expedient."[18] Dividing troops was also acceptable "when great difficulties of terrain have to be overcome or when accurate information of the theatre of war is unobtainable, it is doubtful if the objective can be reached at all by any particular line."[19] On both counts Middleton acted in a manner he could justify within traditions of small wars. The one prerequisite for dividing a troop is that "each faction is strong enough to stand by itself and to hold its own against any force which the enemy will be able to bring against it."[20] That Middleton misjudged. But, as Callwell qualified, "this is where the difficulty arises in planning the campaign, for it is often impossible to foresee how far the opposing forces may be able to assemble in any particular part of the theatre of war."[21] At Fish Creek the success of the Métis guerilla tactics worried Middleton so much that he openly doubted the fighting capacity of his men, and from there on his troop stayed together for what would be the final advance to Batoche.

Middleton appears to have anticipated many of the obstacles he would have to face and it was an awareness that was not particularly remarkable in light of his training and experience. He was solid, not exceptional. He tried to follow his strategy as closely as possible. But for reasons mostly beyond his control, the initiative was briefly lost with the setback at Fish Creek and again after his two-pronged attack on Batoche failed when the ferry cable incapacitated the *Northcote*. Fighting the besieged Métis proved beneficial to Middleton and hid the weakness of his troops from obvious notice.

The odds were with Middleton and his campaign succeeded. Military historian C.P. Stacey has concluded that

> Middleton made a sound appreciation when he decided to direct his main effort against the centre of disaffection at Batoche. This was an example of proper Selection and Maintenance of the Aim. Sound policy, indeed, would have dictated a still heavier concentration against this vital point; but Middleton and the Government were deluged with requests for protection from settlements throughout the West, and political necessity required more dispersion than strictly military consideration would have justified.[22]

At Batoche the end result meant that few looked closely at the means, and the victory of the Field Force glossed over most strategical or tactical weaknesses of the campaign. In discussing Middleton's role, most 20th-century historians have been quick to point to successes of the campaign he led and have emphasized his victory at Batoche. In these histories the last day of fighting at Batoche is detailed but the problems Middleton encountered, particularly on the first day, 9 May, are not fully recounted. Having a more detailed picture of what happened during the Battle of Batoche does not significantly change what has been written about the role Middleton played; what a fuller picture does do is provide a greater awareness and appreciation of how close Middleton was on the first day to suffering severe losses and how fearful he was of his men losing control during the intense fighting. Yet he kept up his soldiers' will to fight through tight situations that might have ended disastrously for his "battle green" men. In the final analysis it was Middleton's battle experience and his knowledge of "small war" tactics that allowed him to engineer a victory.

EPILOGUE

Today we can still walk the ground at Batoche and experience a timeless atmosphere in the wind. We can still walk among the poplar copses that once hid rifle pits. Here and there are reminders of the Métis past: the church, the rectory, the cemetery, the old cellars, remains of trails, and traces of the river-lot system. But little of the battle is in these remnants. The noise of war is gone. Much has been forgotten and lost, much difficult to recover. The Métis and Indians had little reason to recall the event, and they have left few records of it for storytellers, for historians. Their songs were of another past, of the buffalo hunt and the days of the fur trade in Rupert's Land. And the soldiers and

75 Fighting at Batoche. (Saskatchewan Archives Board, R-A 7518.)

reporters, blinded by the emotion of victory, exaggerated their accounts, making "one" story hard to find. Retelling the story would be difficult for future generations; it would have to be built piece by piece from fragments.

But enough was left behind and we now know what happened. We can walk with map in hand down the Humboldt Trail, past Middleton's zareba where 700 raw recruits spent sleepless nights wondering whether they would be trampled by frightened horses. West through the Field Force's shallow rifle pits toward the cemetery, through the bushes where Dakota fire badgered the men in the zareba. Then halfway to the cemetery to the spot where the nine-pounder stood to shell Métis positions on the west side of the river and in the cemetery. And now north across open ground to the church and rectory where Father Moulin's thigh was pierced by an errant bullet, where the wounded soldiers were housed on the first day of fighting, where the bullet holes from Captain Howard's Gatling gun can still be seen. And then toward the river to Mission Ridge where the Métis stopped the soldiers' first advance. Down the gradually sloping hill where Gunner Philips of "A" Battery was killed by Métis returning to their rifle pits after showering shot on the *Northcote*. Here in the pits waited the Métis warriors: Elie Dumont, Rémi Trottier, Athanase Falcon, Ambroise Jobin, Pierre Parenteau, Baptiste Rocheleau, Maxime Lépine, Gilbert Breland, Jean Caron — father and son — André Letendre, Jean Fagnant. It was through these pits that the Midlanders, led by Colonel Williams, broke on the fourth day, running down Mission Ridge toward the village, passing Batoche's house where Donald Ross shot Captain French at a second-storey window. To the river where Alex Fisher lowered the ferry cable that sent the *Northcote*'s smokestacks crashing to its deck. Now returning, back up the Carlton Trail past the village, up the steep slope toward the Jolie Prairie and the line of Métis rifle pits where the Métis met and fought Middleton's men on the third and fourth days. But the manoeuvre was only a feint. The Métis drawn here had weakened their positions at Mission Ridge where the breakthrough came. Now, as we walk south and east, we retrace Middleton's return to the zareba. Back to the zareba where on the fourth day he lost his temper when the coordinated attack had collapsed. Where moments later he rose to follow as the breakthrough was made.

It has been full circle around the vast battlefield, the beautiful site where the Métis settled. And if we pause and look with our minds' eyes, for a moment we will be there again with Riel, Dumont, Middleton, with One Arrow's Cree, White Cap's Dakota, with the shopkeeper from Toronto, the tradesman from Brockville, the Métis from St. Laurent. And if it is a cold spring day, as we listen for the cracking Winchester fire and exploding shells, we will know and feel what happened.

NOTES

Introduction

1   Diane Payment, "Monsieur Batoche," Saskatchewan History, Vol. 32, No. 3 (Autumn 1979), pp. 81-103.

2   The number of men who fought at Batoche is difficult to determine. Depending on the day and source they ranged from 50 to 400. The estimate of 250-300 is based on a letter to Bishop Taché written by P.H. Garnot for the prisoners taken at the battle: "Métis present at Batoche, May 9-12, 1885," Archives de l'archevêché de Saint-Boniface, St. Boniface, Manitoba (hereafter cited as AASB), T, Fonds Taché, lettres reçues. The letter lists 282 Métis participants, all of whom had fought at some time during the four days but not on every day. In addition 35-40 Indians were at Batoche. Together these groups total about 320 men. The estimate of 250-300 likely refers to the first day of the fighting. On the last day Maxime Lépine thought only 50 to 60 men were fighting.

3   Canada. Parliament. House of Commons (hereafter cited as CHC), Sessional Papers, Vol. 13, No. 52 (1886), Queen v. Kahpah-yak-as-to-Kum, p. 13, and Queen v. White Cap, p. 33.

4   Dictionary of Canadian Biography (Toronto: Univ. of Toronto Press, 1966-), Vol. 11, 1881 to 1890, s.v. "Kapeyakwaskonam."

5   See trial evidence in CHC, Sessional Papers, Vol. 13, No. 52 (1886).

6   Some Métis clearly did not support Riel in 1885. See Manitoba. Provincial Archives, MG9, A31, "Mémoires de Louis Schmidt," pp. T31419-21.

7   Petitions forwarded to the federal government from 1878 to 1885 showed a particular concern for these issues. For further discussion of Métis political concerns see Diane Payment, "Batoche, Saskatchewan, 1870-1930: History of a Métis Community," manuscript on file, Prairie Regional Office, Parks Canada, Winnipeg; forthcoming in this series.

8   See the introduction to Desmond Morton, comp., Telegrams of the North-West Campaign, 1885, ed. and intro. Desmond Morton and Reginald H. Roy (Toronto: Champlain Society, 1972) (hereafter cited as Telegrams).

Part I   The Battle of Batoche, 9-12 May 1885

Prelude to Battle

1   Gilbert John Elliot-Murray-Kynynmound, 4th Earl of Minto (formerly Lord Melgund), 'North-West Campaign — 1885,' in Carman Miller, "Lord Melgund and the North-West Campaign of 1885," Saskatchewan History, Vol. 22, No. 3 (Autumn 1969) (hereafter cited as 'Campaign'), p. 97.

2   AASB, Journal de l'abbé Cloutier, 1886 (hereafter cited as Cloutier), (Pierre Henry), p. 5069. The Cloutier collection contains eyewitness accounts of the fighting.

3   Charles Arkoll Boulton, Reminiscences of the North-West Rebellions.... (Toronto: Grip Printing & Publishing, 1886), p. 251.

4   Charles Arkoll Boulton, op. cit., p. 274; Sir Frederick Dobson Middleton, Suppression of the Rebellion in the North West Territories of Canada, 1885, ed. and intro. G.H. Needler (Toronto: Univ. of Toronto Press, 1948), p. 44.

5   Sir Frederick Dobson Middleton, op. cit., p. 44.

6   Charles Pelham Mulvaney, The History of the North-West Rebellion of 1885.... (Toronto: A.H. Hovey, 1885), p. 194. Mulvaney's book should be used with caution for he often quotes others at length without specifying the informant. He was not at Batoche himself.

7   Canada. Public Archives. Manuscript Division (hereafter cited as PAC), MG27, II, B1, Sir Gilbert John Elliot, 4th Earl of Minto, File on the Northwest Rebellion, 1885 (microfilm A-129) (hereafter cited as Minto Papers), 9 May 1885; Charles Arkoll Boulton, op. cit., pp. 499-507; Desmond Morton, The Last War Drum: The North West Campaign of 1885 (Toronto: Hakkert, 1972) (hereafter cited as Last War Drum), p. 178.

8   PAC, Minto Papers, 9 May 1885; Charles Arkoll Boulton, op. cit., pp. 499-507; Desmond Morton, Last War Drum, p. 178.

9   Charles Pelham Mulvaney, op. cit., chap. 22.

10 Charles Arkoll Boulton, op. cit., pp. 261-62.

11 Gilbert John Elliot-Murray-Kynynmound, 4th Earl of Minto, 'Campaign,' p. 98.

12 Sir Frederick Dobson Middleton, op. cit., pp. 44-45.
13 Charles Arkoll Boulton, op. cit., p. 257.
14 Charles Pelham Mulvaney, op. cit., p. 196.
15 Ibid., p. 197.
16 Sir Frederick Dobson Middleton, op. cit., p. 45.
17 PAC, Minto Papers, 9 May 1885.
18 Charles Arkoll Boulton, op. cit., pp. 258-59.
19 PAC, MG29, E103, "Clapp Reminiscences," p. 12.

9 May: Incapacitating the Northcote
1 Smith as cited by Charles Arkoll Boulton, op. cit., p. 490.
2 Smith as cited by Charles Arkoll Boulton, op. cit., p. 491.
3 Charles Pelham Mulvaney, op. cit., p. 225.
4 Sir Frederick Dobson Middleton, op. cit., p. 45.
5 AASB, Cloutier (Fourmond), p. 5084-85.
6 Ibid. (Philippe Garnot), p. 5111.
7 Smith as cited by Charles Arkoll Boulton, op. cit., p. 491.
8 Smith as cited by Charles Pelham Mulvaney, op. cit., p. 226.
9 Charles Pelham Mulvaney, op. cit., p. 225.
10 CHC, Sessional Papers, Vol. 19, No. 5 (1886), p. 41.
11 Charles Pelham Mulvaney, op. cit., pp. 230-31.
12 Saskatchewan. University (Saskatoon), Shortt Library of Canadiana, Morton Collection, MSS C550/1/281.

9 May: Firefight for Mission Ridge
1 Charles Arkoll Boulton, op. cit., p. 260.
2 Charles Pelham Mulvaney, op. cit., p. 199.
3 AASB, Cloutier (Fourmond), pp. 5085-86.
4 Charles Pelham Mulvaney, op. cit., p. 200.
5 Ibid., p. 199.
6 AASB, Cloutier (Fourmond), pp. 5085-86.
7 Sir Frederick Dobson Middleton, op. cit., p. 46.
8 AASB, Cloutier (Fourmond), pp. 5085-86
9 Charles Arkoll Boulton, op. cit., p. 260.
10 Sir Frederick Dobson Middleton, op. cit., p. 46.
11 Ibid.
12 Charles Arkoll Boulton, op. cit., pp. 262.
13 Charles Pelham Mulvaney, op. cit., p. 200.
14 Sir Frederick Dobson Middleton, op. cit., p. 46.
15 Charles Arkoll Boulton, op. cit., pp. 261-62.
16 Sir Frederick Dobson Middleton, op. cit., p. 46.
17 Gilbert John Elliot-Murray-Kynynmound, 4th Earl of Minto, 'Campaign,' p. 104.
18 AASB, Cloutier (Michel Trottier), p. 5141.

9 May: The Métis Offensive
1 AASB, Cloutier (Elie Dumont), pp. 5123-24.
2 Ernest John Chambers, The Royal Grenadiers; A Regimental History of the 10th Infantry Regiment of the Active Militia of Canada.... (Toronto: E.L. Ruddy, 1904), p. 64. See also Gilbert John Elliot-Murray-Kynynmound, 4th Earl of Minto, 'Campaign,' pp. 104-05.
3 Sir Frederick Dobson Middleton, op. cit., p. 46.
4 Charles Pelham Mulvaney, op. cit., p. 206; see also Sir Frederick Dobson Middleton, op. cit., p. 47. Some discrepancies surround the accounts describing troop deployment during the recovery of Philips's body. Middleton wrote that he sent the Midlanders under Lt. Col. Williams down an adjoining ravine. "This was well and boldly done, and Peters, with some of his men, assisted by Dr. Codd of the 90th [Winnipeg Rifles], gallantly went down with the stretcher and brought the man back without further loss; but the poor man was dead." Another reported that the attempted rescue was led by the Midlanders and that the Gatling gun was used to distract the enemy; in this account Peter's actions were deemed worthy of a Victoria Cross.
5 See, for example, Ernest John Chambers, op. cit.; Charles Pelham Mulvaney, op. cit.; PAC, MG29, E103, "Clapp Reminiscences"; and Gilbert John Elliot-Murray-Kynynmound, 4th Earl of Minto, 'Campaign.'
6 Gilbert John Elliot-Murray-Kynynmound, 4th Earl of Minto, 'Campaign,' p. 105. Middleton made almost no mention of being cut off from supplies, but it is detailed at some length in numerous other accounts. See also Charles Pelham Mulvaney, op. cit., p. 201: "For a time we were surrounded by fires from the sloughs, the smoke of which rolled along the ground like dense fog. It was a tight place, but the troops never for a moment flinched. They simply looked to their officers who in turn patiently waited for orders from the chief."
7 Charles Pelham Mulvaney, op. cit., pp. 206-07.
8 Sir Frederick Dobson Middleton, op. cit., p. 47.
9 Gilbert John Elliot-Murray-Kynynmound, 4th Earl of Minto, 'Campaign,' p. 100.
10 PAC, MG27, I, B6, Henry Charles Keith Petty-Fitzmaurice, 5th Marquess of Lansdowne (microfilm A-623) (hereafter cited as Lansdowne Papers), Melgund to Middleton, 21 Feb. 1886.
11 Ibid.
12 Ibid.

9 May: Building the Zareba

1. Sir Charles Edward Callwell, Small Wars. Their Principles and Practice (London: Printed for H.M. Stationery Office by Harrison and Sons, 1896), p. 242.
2. Charles Pelham Mulvaney, op. cit., p. 207.
3. [Lewis Redman Ord], Reminiscences of a Bungle. By One of the Bunglers (Toronto: Grip Printing and Publishing, 1887), p. 13; Saskatchewan Archives Board, Saskatoon, Homestead Files 11184, 645177.
4. H. Haig, "The Canadian North-West Rebellion, 1885," [Part 1], The Royal Engineers Journal, Vol. 26, No. 304 (2 Mar. 1896), p. 68.
5. Ibid., p. 52.
6. [Lewis Redman Ord], op. cit., p. 13.
7. Richard Carnie Laurie, Reminiscences of Early Days in Battleford and with Middleton's Column.... (Battleford: Saskatchewan Herald, 1935), p. 59.
8. Ernest John Chambers, op. cit., p. 68.
9. PAC, MG29, E64, Harold Penryn Rusden, "Notes on the Suppression of the North-West Insurrection," pp. 51-52.
10. Charles Arkoll Boulton, op. cit., p. 267.
11. Charles Pelham Mulvaney, op. cit., p. 214.
12. Arthur O. Wheeler, "The D.L.S. Intelligence Corps and the Riel Rebellion, 1885," The Canadian Surveyor, Vol. 4, No. 12 (April 1934), p. 5.
13. Major Donald James Goodspeed, Battle Royal: A History of the Royal Regiment of Canada, 1862-1962 ([Toronto]: Royal Regiment of Canada Association, [1962]), p. 49.
14. Richard Carnie Laurie, op. cit., p. 58.
15. H. Haig, "The Canadian North-West Rebellion, 1885," [Part 1], The Royal Engineers Journal, Vol. 26, No. 304 (2 Mar. 1896), p. 52.
16. Charles Pelham Mulvaney, op. cit., p. 219.
17. Ibid., p. 252.
18. H. Haig, "The Canadian North-West Rebellion, 1885," [Part 1], The Royal Engineers Journal, Vol. 26, No. 304 (2 Mar. 1896), p. 68.
19. Sir Frederick Dobson Middleton, op. cit., p. 48.
20. Charles Pelham Mulvaney, op. cit., p. 207.
21. Ibid.
22. PAC, MG29, E64, Harold Rusden, "Notes on the Suppression," p. 51.
23. Ibid., p. 52.
24. Charles Pelham Mulvaney, op. cit., p. 208.
25. Ernest John Chambers, op. cit., p. 68.
26. Ibid.
27. Ibid.
28. AASB, Cloutier (Fourmond), p. 5089.
29. Ibid. (Elie Dumont), p. 5125.
30. Ibid. (Fourmond), p. 5095.
31. Ibid., p. 5088.
32. Ibid., p. 5095.
33. Ibid. (Baptiste Vandale), p. 5113.
34. Ibid., p. 5111.
35. Charles Pelham Mulvaney, op. cit., pp. 202-04.

10 and 11 May : A Plan Developes

1. PAC, MG29, E103, "Clapp Reminiscences," p. 13.
2. Charles Pelham Mulvaney, op. cit., p. 210.
3. Sir Frederick Dobson Middleton, op. cit., p. 48; AASB, Cloutier (Fourmond), p. 5092.
4. PAC, MG29, E103, "Clapp Reminiscences," p. 13.
5. H. Haig, "The Canadian North-West Rebellion, 1885," [Part 2], The Royal Engineers Journal, Vol. 26, No. 305 (1 Apr. 1896), p. 68.
6. Charles Pelham Mulvaney, p. 252.
7. Ibid., pp. 210-11.
8. Garnet Joseph Wolseley, 1st Viscount Wolseley, The Soldier's Pocket-book for Field Service (London: MacMillan and Co., 1869), p. 225.
9. Sir Frederick Dobson Middleton, op. cit., p. 48.
10. Charles Arkoll Boulton, op. cit., p. 269.
11. Charles Pelham Mulvaney, op. cit., p. 211.
12. Sir Frederick Dobson Middleton, op. cit., p. 49.
13. Ibid.
14. Charles Arkoll Boulton, op. cit., p. 270.
15. Charles Pelham Mulvaney, op. cit., p. 213.
16. AASB, Cloutier (Fourmond), p. 5091.
17. CHC, Sessional Papers, Vol. 19, No. 5 (1886), p. 30.
18. Sir Frederick Dobson Middleton, op. cit., p. 80; Charles Arkoll Boulton, op. cit., p. 272.
19. Sir Frederick Dobson Middleton, op. cit., p. 50.
20. Ibid.
21. Ibid.
22. Charles Arkoll Boulton, op. cit., p. 273.
23. CHC, Sessional Papers, Vol. 19, No. 5 (1886), p. 31.
24. Sir Frederick Dobson Middleton, op. cit., p. 50.

12 May: The Final Day

1. Sir Frederick Dobson Middleton, op. cit., pp. 50-51.
2. Charles Arkoll Boulton, op. cit., p. 275.
3. Charles Pelham Mulvaney, op. cit., p. 257.

4   CHC, Sessional Papers, Vol. 19, No. 5 (1886), p. 31.
5   Charles Arkoll Boulton, op. cit., pp. 277-78.
6   Sir Frederick Dobson Middleton, op. cit., p. 51.
7   CHC, Sessional Papers, Vol. 19, No. 5 (1886), p. 31.
8   Charles Pelham Mulvaney, op. cit., p. 257.
9   Desmond Morton, comp., Telegrams, p. lxii.
10 AASB, Cloutier (Maxime Lépine), p. 5120; ibid. (Baptiste Richolet), p. 5111.
11 Ibid. (Baptiste Vandale), p. 5114.
12 Ibid.
13 Ibid. (Antoine Ferguson), pp. 5106-09.
14 Ibid. (Fourmond), p. 5097.
15 Ibid. (Joseph Ouellette), pp. 5133-34.
16 Charles Pelham Mulvaney, op. cit., p. 257.
17 Charles Arkoll Boulton, op. cit., p. 259.
18 CHC, Sessional Papers, Vol. 19, No. 5 (1886), p. 33.
19 Charles Pelham Mulvaney, op. cit., p. 221.
20 Ibid., p. 216.
21 Sir Frederick Dobson Middleton, op. cit., p. 52.
22 Ibid., pp. 52.
23 Ibid., pp. 52-3.
24 Charles Pelham Mulvaney, op. cit., p. 292.
25 Ibid., pp. 292-93.
26 Charles Arkoll Boulton, op. cit., p. 285.
27 Sir Frederick Dobson Middleton, op. cit., p. 53.
28 Ibid., p. 53.
29 Charles Pelham Mulvaney, op. cit., p. 284.
30 Ibid., p. 277.
31 Ibid.
32 Ibid.
33 PAC, RG15, Department of the Interior, Rebellion Losses, Vol. 928, p. 708.
34 Charles Pelham Mulvaney, op. cit., p. 268.
35 AASB, Cloutier (Elie Dumont), p. 5159.
36 The Riel Rebellions, A Cartographic History/Le récit cartographique des affaires Riel, comp. William A. Oppen, (Toronto: Univ. of Toronto Press in assoc. with Public Archives Canada and Canadian Government Publishing Centre, 1979), p. 73.

After the Battle

1   Norma Sluman and Jean Goodwill, John Tootoosis, Biography of a Cree Leader (Ottawa: Golden Dog Press, 1982), p. 40.
2   Charles Pelham Mulvaney, op. cit., p. 275.
3   Charles Arkoll Boulton, op. cit., p. 288.
4   Charles Pelham Mulvaney, op. cit., p. 276.
5   Ibid., p. 286.

6   Ibid., p. 275.
7   Sir Frederick Dobson Middleton, op. cit., p. 53.
8   Ibid., p. xvii.
9   PAC, Minto Papers, Vol. 7, Lansdowne to Melgund, 30 April 1885.
10 PAC, Lansdowne Papers, Lansdowne to Lord Derby, 17 April 1885.
11 Gilbert John Elliot-Murray-Kynynmound, 4th Earl of Minto, 'Campaign,' p. 86.

Part II: Leadership and Military Traditions

Riel and Dumont: The Strategy to Defend Batoche

1   Isaac Cowie, The Company of Adventurers; A Narrative of Seven Years in the Service of the Hudson's Bay Company during 1867-1874.... (Toronto: W. Briggs, 1913), p. 170.
2   Robert Harry Lowie, Indians of the Plains (Toronto: McGraw-Hill, 1954), pp. 104-12. For Métis military traditions see Margaret Arnett MacLeod and W.L. Morton, Cuthbert Grant of Grantown: Warden of the Plains of Red River (Toronto: McClelland and Stewart, 1974), especially chaps. 4 and 8.
3   For example, George Woodcock, Gabriel Dumont: The Métis Chief and His Lost World (Edmonton: Hurtig, 1975); George Francis Gilman Stanley, Louis Riel (Toronto: Ryerson, 1963); Peter B. Waite, Canada 1874-1896; Arduous Destiny (Toronto: McClelland and Stewart, 1971); Desmond Morton, comp., Telegrams.
4   Gabriel Dumont as cited in The Other Natives: The Métis, ed. Antoine S. Lussier and D. Bruce Sealey, authors T.J. Brasser et al. (Winnipeg: Manitoba Métis Federation Press, 1978-), Vol. 1, p. 157.
5   E.R. Markson et al., "The Life and Death of Louis Riel, A Study in Forensic Psychiatry," Canadian Psychiatric Association Journal, Vol. 10, No. 4 (Aug. 1965), p. 249. See also a more recent psychiatric assessment by S.K. Littman, "A Pathography of Louis Riel," Canadian Psychiatric Association Journal, Vol. 23, No. 7 (1978), p. 461. Littman generally agrees with Markson et al. that Riel suffered rather severe mental disturbances.
6   AASB, Cloutier (Fourmond), p. 93.
7   PAC, MG26, G, Rt. Hon. Sir Wilfred Laurier, Political Papers, Correspondence, Vol. 2 (hereafter cited as Laurier Papers), Alex Fisher, p. 687.
8   E.R. Markson et al., op. cit., p. 248.
9   See, for example, George Woodcock, op. cit., pp. 162-63.

10   PAC, Laurier Papers, Alex Fisher, p. 676.
11   Peter B. Waite, op. cit., p. 89.
12   PAC, Laurier Papers, Alex Fisher, p. 686.
13   Louis Riel, The Diaries of Louis Riel, ed. Thomas Flanagan (Edmonton: Hurtig, 1979), pp. 74-75. Some evidence exists of more temporal concerns. Much of it is difficult to reconcile to Riel's religious schemes. See, for example, Queen's University Archives, Kingston, Ont., George H. Young, Notebook, recording Riel's comments after his capture: "General plan of defence mine. Special credit due to G. Dumont. My reserves I placed as to be an attack on 2 roads at once. G. Dumont though our right the key. The Artillery Fire kept men from advancing if not for the fire they would have gone at your line and stopped it."
14   George Woodcock, op. cit., p. 170.

Tactics of The Métis
1   Margaret Arnett MacLeod and W.L. Morton, op. cit., p. 112.
2   Robert Harry Lowie, op. cit., p. 104.
3   Margaret Arnett MacLeod and W.L. Morton, op. cit., p. 145.
4   Alexander Henry, "Henry's Journal, Covering Adventures and Experiences in the Fur Trade on the Red River, 1799-1801 ... by Charles N. Bell," Historical and Scientific Society of Manitoba Transaction, No. 31 (1888), p. 5.
5   "Trenches at Flee Island," Sioux Press (Vermillion, South Dakota), 13 May 1948.
6   CHC, Sessional Papers, Vol. 13, No. 52 (1886), Department of Militia and Defence, Pl. X.
7   John Frederick Charles Fuller, The Conduct of War, 1789-1961; A Study of the Impact of the French, Industrial and Russian Revolutions on War and its Conduct (London: Eyre Methuen, 1961), p. 104.
8   Ibid., pp. 104-05.
9   Ibid., pp. 105.

Middleton and the North-West Field Force
1   Hugh Thomas, The Story of Sandhurst (London: Hutchinson, 1961), p. 37.
2   Desmond Morton, Ministers and Generals; Politics and the Canadian Militia, 1868-1904 (Toronto: Univ. of Toronto Press, 1970) (hereafter cited as Ministers), chap. 4.
3   George Taylor Denison, Soldiering in Canada: Recollections and Experiences..., 2nd ed. (Toronto: George N. Morang, 1901), p. 103.

4   Ibid., p. 340.
5   Ibid. Denison was awarded the top prize in a competition commissioned by the Imperial Government of Russia for his History of the Cavalry.
6   I am indebted to Jack Summers for pointing this out.
7   George Taylor Denison, op. cit., chap. 23.
8   Sir Frederick Dobson Middleton, op. cit., p. 15.
9   Ibid., p. xiv.
10   George Francis Gilman Stanley, op. cit., p. 272.
11   Ibid., p. 378.
12   Desmond Morton, comp., Telegrams, p. xxx.
13   Quoted in ibid., p. xxxiii.
14   C.F. Hamilton, "The Canadian Militia: The Northwest Rebellion, 1885," Canadian Defence Quarterly, Vol. 7, No. 2 (Jan. 1930), p. 222.
15   Col. Charles P. Stacey, ed., Introduction to the Study of Military History for Canadian Students, 5th ed., 2nd rev. (Ottawa: Queen's Printer, 1960), pp. 84-85.

Middleton's Tactics in Retrospect
1   See George Taylor Denison, op. cit., chaps. 20-23, and George Francis Gilman Stanley, op. cit., p. 356.
2   Garnet Joseph Wolseley, 1st Viscount Wolseley, op. cit., pp. 223-25.
3   Sir Charles Edward Callwell, op. cit.
4   Ibid., p. 1.
5   Ibid., p. 12.
6   Ibid., p. 21.
7   Ibid., p. 51.
8   Ibid.
9   Ibid., p. 63.
10   Ibid., p. 196.
11   Ibid.
12   Ibid., pp. 204-05.
13   Desmond Morton, Ministers, pp. 207-24.
14   Sir Charles Edward Callwell, op. cit., pp. 240-41.
15   Ibid., p. 240.
16   Ibid., pp. 244, 264.
17   Ibid., p. 88.
18   Ibid., p. 89.
19   Ibid.
20   Ibid., pp. 91.
21   Ibid., pp. 91-92.
22   Col. Charles P. Stacey, ed., op. cit., p. 84.

SELECT BIBLIOGRAPHY

Boulton, Charles Arkoll
Reminiscences of the North-West Rebellions.... Grip Printing and Publishing, Toronto, 1886.

Callwell, Sir Charles Edward
Small Wars. Their Principles and Practice. Printed for H.M. Stationery Office by Harrison and Sons, London, 1896.

Cameron, William Bleasdell
Blood Red the Sun. 4th ed. rev. Kenway Publishing, Calgary, 1950.

Chambers, Ernest John
The Royal Grenadiers; A Regimental History of the 10th Infantry Regiment of the Active Militia of Canada.... E.L. Ruddy, Toronto, 1904.

Denison, George Taylor
Soldiering in Canada; Recollections and Experiences.... 2nd ed. George N. Morang, Toronto, 1901.

De Trémaudan, Auguste Henri
Histoire de la nation métisse dans l'ouest Canadien. Albert Lévesque, Montreal, [1936].
The History of the Métis Nation in Western Canada. Abridged and trans. A. Thomas. Métis Historical Society, Winnipeg, n.d.

Jefferson, Robert
Fifty Years on the Saskatchewan; Being a History of Cree Indian Domestic Life and Difficulties.... Canadian Northwest Historical Society, Battleford, Sask., [1929]. Canadian Northwest Historical Society Publications, Vol. 1, No. 5.

MacLeod, Margaret Arnett, and W.L. Morton
Cuthbert Grant of Grantown: Warden of the Plains of Red River. McClelland and Stewart, Toronto, 1974.

Morton, Desmond
Canada and War: A Military and Political History. Butterworths, Toronto, 1981.
"Des Canadiens errants: French Canadian Troops in the North West Campaign of 1885." Journal of Canadian Studies, Vol. 5, No. 3 (Aug. 1970), pp. 28-39.
The Last War Drum; The North West Campaign of 1885. Hakkert, Toronto, 1972.
Ministers and Generals; Politics and the Canadian Militia, 1868-1904. University of Toronto Press, Toronto, 1970.

Morton, Desmond, comp.
Telegrams of the North-West Campaign, 1885. Ed. and intro. Desmond Morton and Reginald H. Roy. Champlain Society, Toronto, 1972.

The Other Natives: The Métis
Ed. Antoine S. Lussier and D. Bruce Sealey; T.J. Brasser et al., authors. Manitoba Métis Federation Press, Winnipeg, 1978-. Vol. 1: 1700-1885.

The Riel Rebellions, A Cartographic History/Le récit cartographique des affaires Riel
Comp. William A. Oppen. University of Toronto Press, Toronto, in association with the Public Archives Canada and the Canadian Government Publishing Centre, 1979.

BIBLIOGRAPHY

Stacey, Colonel Charles P.
"The North-West Campaign, 1885." <u>Canadian Army Journal</u>, Vol. 8, No. 3 (July 1954), pp. 10-20.

Stacey, Colonel Charles P., ed.
<u>Introduction to the Study of Military History for Canadian Students</u>. 5th ed., 2nd rev. Queen's Printer, Ottawa, 1960.

Stanley, George Francis Gilman
"Gabriel Dumont's Account of the North West Rebellion, 1885." <u>Canadian Historical Review</u>, Vol. 30, No. 3 (Sept. 1949), pp. 249-69. Toronto.

Woodcock, George
<u>Gabriel Dumont: The Métis Chief and His Lost World</u>. Hurtig, Edmonton, 1975.